Essays in Post-Critical Philosophy of Technology

Edited by
Mihály Héder
Budapest University of Technology and Economics
(BUTE), Hungary

Eszter Nádasi
Budapest University of Technology and Economics
(BUTE), Hungary

Series in Philosophy

VERNON PRESS

Copyright 2019 by the Authors.

All rights reserved. No part of this publication may be reproduced, stored in a retrieval system, or transmitted in any form or by any means, electronic, mechanical, photocopying, recording, or otherwise, without the prior permission of Vernon Art and Science Inc.

www.vernonpress.com

In the Americas:
Vernon Press
1000 N West Street,
Suite 1200, Wilmington,
Delaware 19801
United States

In the rest of the world:
Vernon Press
C/Sancti Espiritu 17,
Malaga, 29006
Spain

Series in Philosophy

Library of Congress Control Number: 2018962655

ISBN: 978-1-62273-669-0

Also available:

Hardback: 978-1-62273-457-3

E-book: 978-1-62273-565-5

Cover design by Vernon Press using elements designed by Kotkoa / Freepik.

Product and company names mentioned in this work are the trademarks of their respective owners. While every care has been taken in preparing this work, neither the authors nor Vernon Art and Science Inc. may be held responsible for any loss or damage caused or alleged to be caused directly or indirectly by the information contained in it.

Every effort has been made to trace all copyright holders, but if any have been inadvertently overlooked the publisher will be pleased to include any necessary credits in any subsequent reprint or edition.

Table of contents

Preface — v

Part I - The Role of Technology — 1

Chapter 1 — **Essays on The Role of Technology** — 3

Chapter 2 — **The Role of Technological Knowledge in Scientific Change** — 5

Chapter 3 — **Technology as an Aspect of Human Praxis** — 19

Part II - Post-Critical Philosophy of Technology — 33

Chapter 4 — **Essays on Post-Critical Philosophy of Technology** — 35

Chapter 5 — **Michael Polanyi on Machines as Comprehensive Entities** — 37

Chapter 6 — **Michael Polanyi and the Epistemology of Engineering** — 63

Part III - Aesthetic Approaches — 71

Chapter 7 — **Essays on Aesthetic Approaches** — 73

Chapter 8 — **The Screen: a Body Without Organs** — 75

Chapter 9 — **Techno-Aesthetics and Technics of the Body From Merleau-Ponty to Simondon and Back** — 89

	Part IV - Applications of Philosophy on Technology	99
Chapter 10	**Essays on Applications of Philosophy on Technology**	101
Chapter 11	**Did Mirrors Determine Caravaggio?**	109
Chapter 12	**Nudging for Hyperreality: A Philosophical Study of Technological Choice Architectures**	115
Chapter 13	**Technology-based Critical Phenomena: a Borgmannian Approach of Crisis Prediction**	123
Chapter 14	**The Problem of Undermined Evidence: Accurate Entitlement for Epistemic Systems in Automatic Decision Support Systems**	135
References		*149*
Index		*163*

Preface

This book grew out of an event titled Budapest Workshop on Philosophy of Technology, held 1-2 December 2017.

The workshop was a great success with authors from **USA**, **Japan**, **Canada**, **Portugal**, **Italy**, **France**, **Belgium**, **Russia**, **Norway**, the **United Kingdom** and **Kazakhstan**.

Authors from Hungary represented almost all major institutions of the field: Hungarian Academy of Science's Institute for Computer Science and Control (**MTA SZTAKI**) - a Fraunhofer Project Center; Budapest University of Technology and Economics (**BME**); Central European University (**CEU**); Eötvös Lóránd University (**ELTE**).

The event was a vibrant, highly successful one with many ideas exchanged between the participants. About half of them have subsequently written an article for this book.

This book is divided into four parts. Part I, *The Role of Technology*, sets up the perspective for all the remaining chapters. Both pieces in this part deal with the place of technology in intellectual history (in a very broad sense), but they apply a very different approach.

Part II, *Post-Critical Philosophy of Technology*, refers to a particular epistemic stance towards understanding the world, one that attempts to move beyond the rigidity of the past approaches. Both papers here investigate the famous philosopher of science, Michael Polanyi's works and their consequences for philosophy of technology. While Polanyi coined the term "post-critical" which we are using in the title of our book; this attitude is by no means limited to his works.

Aesthetic Approaches, part III of this book is a nice example of how we might use the term post-critical in a broad sense: the two chapters in this part start from the phenomenology of the body and make contact with technology and the novel experience it brings to our lives.

Finally, in part IV, *Applications of Philosophy on Technology*, the reader will find a variety of cases in which our authors apply a philosophical approach to contemporary problems, including Decision Support Systems, Crisis Communication, Choice Architectures and intriguing problems in the history of art.

Acknowledgement: This volume was supported by the János Bolyai Research Scholarship of the Hungarian Academy of Sciences and the ÚNKP-18-4 New National Excellence Program of the Ministry of Human Capacities.

Part I - The Role of Technology

Chapter 1

Essays on The Role of Technology

Mihály Héder

This book starts with two essays that provide a bird's-eye view of technology.

Barseghyan & Mirkin are discussing technology's role in Scientonomy, the empirical science of scientific change itself. Their central claim is that

> "there is accepted propositional technological knowledge which plays an indispensable role in the process of scientific change."

However, technological knowledge has been underserved by the field of intellectual history - which then results in a gap in our understanding of change, especially scientific change. They investigate whether the reason for this negligence is in part the nature of technological knowledge. On this track, they touch on the partially tacit nature of technology, which will be a recurring topic in this book.

In their excellent work, they characterize technological knowledge in terms of epistemology, drawing on several important authors.

Laszlo Ropolyi also deals with technology as the possible driver behind change, but at a more abstract level. In his quest to characterize the nature of technology, he offers a very helpful review of approaches by several distinguished philosophers of technology.

In his overarching approach, he is able to locate his stance relative to Heidegger and Ellul, the SCOT approach, Feenberg, Marcuse, Foucault and Ihde.

He concludes that:

> "... hermeneutics, social constructivism, and postmodern philosophical systems are systems of the philosophy of technology as well since they necessarily include the possibility of interpreting technology philosophically, though of course only in an implicit form, or using a Hegelian term, in an unhappy form." (...) "Given the above conceptualization of technology, it is evident that technology has primacy over intellectual practices such as do-

ing philosophy or doing science. This is because being a human is prerequisite for being a philosopher or for being a scientist."

This characterization of technology sets the tone nicely for the other three parts of our book.

Chapter 2

The Role of Technological Knowledge in Scientific Change

Hakob Barseghyan and Maxim Mirkin

Institute for the History and Philosophy of Science and Technology, University of Toronto

Summary

The current scientonomic discourse focuses largely on theories and methods of natural, social, and formal *sciences*, while the role of *technological* knowledge in the process of scientific change is virtually neglected. This neglect, we argue, has to do with the scientonomic distinction between two epistemic stances – *acceptance* of a theory as the best available description of its domain and its *use* in practical applications. The view that is implicit in contemporary *scientonomy* is that sciences alone can produce *accepted* knowledge, while technologies are all about knowledge *use*. In contrast, we argue that there is *accepted* propositional technological knowledge which plays an indispensable role in the process of scientific change. We demonstrate that technological disciplines do not merely *use* theories but also produce *accepted* theories, such as "x is an effective treatment for medical condition y", "z is a viable technology for bridge-building", and "p is a statistically valid technique for assessing public opinion about q". There are both theoretical and historical reasons to believe that changes in technological knowledge exhibit the same patterns as changes in natural, social, and formal sciences. In addition, technological knowledge is intrinsically intertwined with scientific knowledge as accepted scientific and technological theories often jointly shape employed methods.

2.1 Introduction

As a descriptive empirical science, scientonomy attempts to describe and explain the process of scientific change. Like any empirical science, it has two intertwined sides – theoretical and observational. The goal of theoretical scientonomy is to uncover the *general* patterns of scientific change, while the goal of observational scientonomy is to reconstruct the mosaics (the belief systems) of *theories* and *methods* (criteria) of theory evaluation of *individual* epistemic communities and explain changes in them.[1] Recent developments in theoretical scientonomy[2] have created a distinct possibility for developing a quantitative and qualitative database of intellectual history, the *Tree of Knowledge*[3] that will serve as a centralized clearing house for scholarly knowledge on different epistemic communities and their belief systems. By documenting the scholarly consensus concerning the content of different historical mosaics, the database will also reveal the gaps in our historical record and, thus, invite future research. In its ambition, the Tree of Knowledge project is on the same scale of complexity as the analogous projects in other fields, such as astronomical catalogues, the biological tree of life, and the database of religious history.

Since any database requires a detailed *ontology* of types of entities and relations which presumably populate the respective domain and which the database is expected to document, clarifying the ontology of scientific change is one of the prerequisites of the database of intellectual history.[4] Normally, scientific databases draw their ontologies from theoretical branches of their respective sciences: the structure of tables, fields, and relations of the phylogenetic tree of life database is dictated by our current theoretical biology, just as the taxonomy of any astronomical database is informed by our current astronomical theories. By the same token, the structure of the database of intellectual history is to be drawn from our current scientonomic knowledge concerning the ontology of scientific change, i.e. our knowledge concerning the types of epistemic *agents*, *entities*, and *stances* that one finds in the pro-

---

[1] Note that, in the scientonomic context, the words "method" and "criteria" are used interchangeably; they both denote the rules for employment in theory evaluation.

[2] At the moment, there are four axioms and more than twenty theorems accepted in scientonomy. Collectively these axioms and theorems explain different aspects of the process of scientific change, including theory acceptance, method employment, scientific inertia, compatibility, underdetermination, role of sociocultural factors, splitting and merging of mosaics, authority delegation, and more. For the current state of theoretical scientonomy, refer to the Encyclopedia of Scientonomy at www.scientowiki.com/Community:Scientonomy.

[3] The name, the *Tree of Knowledge*, is dictated by the database's aim to become for the history of knowledge what the biological Tree of Life database has become for the evolutionary history of biological species. See www.scientowiki.com/Tree_of_Knowledge_Project for details.

[4] In this context, "ontology" denotes a description of the entities and relations that populate a certain domain.

cess of scientific change.[5] While there are still many open questions concerning the ontology of scientific change, it is important to appreciate that no database of intellectual history is possible without a well-articulated and accepted ontology of scientific change.

So far, the discussions concerning the scientonomic foundations of the database have almost exclusively focused on *scientific* theories and methods.[6] The primary focus of the scientonomic discourse has been on tracing and explaining changes in natural, social, and formal *sciences*. As for *technological knowledge*, it has been virtually absent from scientonomic discourse. We find this state of affairs unfortunate, as it is clear to us that mosaics of epistemic communities can contain not only accepted scientific theories but also a vast layer of accepted technological knowledge. Thus, we claim that there *is* accepted technological knowledge which plays an indispensable role in the process of scientific change.

We will start by identifying the roots of this exclusion and clarifying why *technological* knowledge has been left out of scientonomic discourse. Then, in the second section, we will discuss the notion of *technological knowledge* and will outline the important difference between *explicit, explicable-implicit*, and *inexplicable* knowledge. We will then refine our main thesis and show that accepted *propositional* technological knowledge – both explicit and explicable-implicit – plays an indispensable role in the process of scientific change. There are two main reasons for supporting this thesis. First, it has already been suggested that changes in technological knowledge seem to exhibit the same patterns as changes in *scientific* theories and methods [127]. In this paper, we will focus on the second of the two reasons: the fact that technological knowledge is intrinsically *intertwined* with scientific knowledge. In particular, we will demonstrate how both our accepted *technological* theories and our accepted *scientific* theories often jointly shape our methods of theory evaluation. We will conclude by stating that no scientonomic reconstruction of a historical mosaic would be complete without proper attention to the technological propositions accepted in that mosaic.

---

[5] For a detailed exposition of the current scientonomic views on the ontology of scientific change, refer to the respective section of the encyclopedia at www.scientowiki.com/Ontology_of_Scientific_Change.

[6] Several directions are currently being pursued by scientonomists. One recently accepted suggestion is to include *questions* into the ontology of scientific change as a separate epistemic entity [179].

2.2 Why has Technological Knowledge been Neglected?

In the scientonomic context, the question concerning the status of technological knowledge within a scientific mosaic of accepted theories and employed methods was first articulated by Sean Cohmer during the Scientonomy Seminar of 2015.[7] Cohmer pointed out that the mosaic of a typical epistemic community contains a whole layer of technological know-how that is virtually absent from our scientonomic analysis. Subsequently, this led to the formulation of an open question concerning the status of technological knowledge.[8] This paper is essentially an attempt to settle that question.

It is assumed by scientonomists that in order for technological knowledge to be included in the ontology of scientific change it must be shown that, first, there is such a thing as *accepted* technological knowledge and, second, that changes in this accepted technological knowledge obey the same *laws* of scientific change as changes in other parts of a mosaic.[9] Therefore, to proceed, we need to begin with the scientonomic distinction between *acceptance*, *use*, and *pursuit*.

According to the currently accepted ontology of epistemic stances, there are three distinct attitudes that an epistemic community can take towards a theory. A community can *accept* a theory as the best available description or prescription of something [195]. A community can also find a theory *useful* in practical applications. Finally, a community can find a theory *pursuit-worthy*, i.e., worthy of further elaboration [4:p31]. Importantly, these three stances are independent of each other: an accepted theory may or may not also be used in practice, while a used theory may or may not also be accepted as the best description of its domain. An engineer, for example, may accept general relativity but choose to build a bridge using classical physics.[10] Here are the current definitions of the three stances:

---

[7] See www.scientowiki.com/Scientonomy_Seminar_2015.
[8] See www.scientowiki.com/The_Status_of_Technological_Knowledge.
[9] For the laws of scientific change, see [4, 195, 150]. For current scientonomic views on the mechanism of theory acceptance and method employment www.scientowiki.com/Mechanism_of_Theory_Acceptance and www.scientowiki.com/Mechanism_of_Method_Employment.
[10] For an application of this taxonomy to some classical debates in philosophy of science, see [3].

Acceptance ≡	Use ≡	Pursuit ≡
A theory is said to be accepted if it is taken as the best available description or prescription of its object.	A theory is said to be used if it is taken as an adequate tool for practical application.	A theory is said to be pursued if it is considered worthy of further development.

The view implicit in contemporary scientonomy is that scientific fields produce both accepted and used theories, whereas technological disciplines merely *use* theories without producing any *accepted* knowledge of their own. As this view is not explicitly stated in scientonomy, it's hard to say why it became tacitly accepted in the first place. One possible hypothesis is that perhaps it stems from the appreciation of the basic difference between the goals of the two enterprises, for "whereas science aims to understand the world as it is, technology aims to change the world" [54]. Perhaps the fact that technology ultimately aims at changing the world rather than studying it was taken to also imply that technology doesn't produce any knowledge of its own.

In any event, we wish to challenge the view that technology is all about theory *use*. We believe that there is *accepted* technological knowledge and that technological knowledge plays an indispensable role in the process of changes in scientific theories and methods.

2.3 What is Technological Knowledge?

Before we proceed, we need to clarify what *technological knowledge* is. It is clear that *technological knowledge* does not necessarily equal *tacit knowledge*. Moreover, it is evident that the category of *tacit knowledge* is not properly suited to capture the diversity of types of knowledge produced by technologies. There are at least two considerations here.

On the one hand, there is clearly a vast layer of *explicit* knowledge in any technology. This includes both substantive and operative theories, to use Bunge's language [22, 331]. When an engineer claims that "x is a viable bridge building technology", she doesn't merely apply the laws of classical physics to a real-life situation but also produces new knowledge on the design, construction, and operation of a bridge [221] – knowledge that *can be* and often *is* explicitly stated. It is safe to say that most technologies do produce such explicit knowledge, which is normally collected in respective textbooks, manuals, guidelines, handbooks, etc. Any engineering textbook will likely contain a plethora of accepted technological theories; the same goes for medical handbooks, agricultural manuals, statutory guidelines, etc. Thus, it is often the case that technological knowledge is explicitly stated and well-documented.

On the other hand, the category of *tacit* knowledge itself is too broad and imprecise to capture the difference between knowledge that is currently tacit but can in principle be explicated as a set of propositions and knowledge that is inexplicable even in principle. The tradition going back to Polanyi focuses on the distinction between *explicit* and *tacit*. This traditional vocabulary doesn't appreciate the difference between knowledge that is inexplicable *in principle* and knowledge that is *not yet explicated* but can in principle be explicated. Polanyi's own examples reveal that his interest was primarily with the former kind of tacit knowledge – the knowledge that cannot be explicated propositionally even in principle [175]. What remains underappreciated is that any technology will likely contain tacit knowledge that *can* be expressed propositionally. When the first precise marine chronometers for finding longitude at sea were designed in the 18th century, the intricacies of their design and construction would mostly remain tacit knowledge of a select group of craftsmen such as John Harrison [204]. Yet, this is precisely a type of knowledge that *could be* explicated propositionally; it *has been* later on explicated by the likes of Rupert Thomas Gould [66]. Since it is important to distinguish between what is *explicable-implicit* and what is *inexplicable* in principle, what we need is a threefold distinction, like the one summarized in the following table:

❓ Can it be, in principle, formulated as a set of proposition?		
Yes		No
❓ Has it been openly formulated by the community?		**Inexplicable:** Non-propositional knowledge, i.e. knowledge that cannot, even in principle, be formulated as a set of propositions.
Yes	No	
Explicit: Propositional knowledge that has been openly formulated by the community.	**Explicable-Implicit:** Propositional knowledge that hasn't been openly formulated by the community.	

The distinction between these three categories – *explicit, explicable-implicit,* and *inexplicable* – is important as they may turn out to exhibit very different patterns of change. Whether they, in fact, do exhibit different patterns of change is not at issues here; what is important is that any viable taxonomy of types of technological knowledge should account for that hypothetical possibility.

This three-fold distinction is evidently richer than the traditional distinction between *explicit* and *tacit*, as well as between *propositional* and *non-propositional* knowledge.[11] Both explicable-implicit and inexplicable are sub-types of tacit knowledge, while explicit and explicable-implicit are both sub-types of propositional knowledge as they are both expressible propositionally. The following table shows how the traditional dichotomies map on the new three-fold distinction:

❓ Can it be, in principle, formulated as a set of proposition?		
Yes		No
❓ Has it been openly formulated by the community?		**Inexplicable:** Non-propositional knowledge, i.e. knowledge that cannot, even in principle, be formulated as a set of propositions.
Yes	No	
Explicit: Propositional knowledge that has been openly formulated by the community.	**Explicable-Implicit:** Propositional knowledge that hasn't been openly formulated by the community.	
Explicit	Tacit/Implicit	
Propositional		Non-Propositional

Specifically, what the new three-fold distinction highlights is the difference between propositional and non-propositional knowledge; the latter is especially vital for our current discussion, as in this paper we will focus exclusively on *propositional* technological knowledge – both explicit and explicable-implicit. The main reason underlying this decision is the fact that the current laws of scientonomy only deal with propositional knowledge; the very definition of *theory* as a set of propositions [195], currently accepted in scientonomy, suggests that the scientonomic laws currently only apply to changes in those beliefs and norms which can at least in principle be expressed through propositions.

As for the category of *inexplicable* (non-propositional) knowledge, its very existence seems to be the main question separating *intellectualists* and *anti-intellectualists* – a debate that can be traced all the way to Gilbert Ryle [189]. Specifically, there is a debate whether there is such a thing as a genuine

---

[11] Note that here "propositional" is understood as "capable of being expressed through propositions", i.e. as a dispositional property.

knowledge that is in principle not expressible through propositions, or whether that type of "know-how" should be properly classified as a skill, rather than knowledge [46]. As our focus in this paper is on *propositional* technological knowledge, we won't be taking any stance on the existence or non-existence of inexplicable knowledge. In any event, since at the moment theoretical scientonomy only deals with propositional knowledge, in our analysis, we focus on *propositional* technological knowledge. Therefore, our main thesis needs to be clarified. We argue *that there is an accepted propositional technological knowledge that is an indispensable part of the process of scientific change*.[12]

The idea that technologies are capable of producing their own specific accepted theories is very much in tune with what some authors have already alluded to. Both Vincenti and Franssen *et al.* have emphasized the existence of explicable technological knowledge that is more than mere applied science. According to Franssen *et al.* "an important input for the design process is scientific knowledge: knowledge about the behavior of components and the materials they are composed of in specific circumstances. This is the point where science is applied. However, much of this knowledge is not directly available from the sciences, since it often concerns extremely detailed behavior in very specific circumstances. This scientific knowledge is therefore often generated within technology, by the engineering sciences" [54]. Similarly, Vincenti has argued that "technology, though it may *apply* science, is not the same as or entirely *applied* science" [221:p4], in particular, due to the fact that technology produces accepted knowledge of its own.

2.4 Why is Propositional Technological Knowledge Indispensable?

There are two main reasons to believe that accepted propositional technological knowledge plays an indispensable role in the process of scientific change. First, propositional technological knowledge exhibits the same *patterns* of change as scientific knowledge. Second, propositional technological knowledge is intrinsically *intertwined* with scientific knowledge.

The former reason has already been discussed in detail by one of the authors of this paper, who showed that, when observing the process of changes in technological beliefs, we notice the same patterns of change as we observe in the process of scientific change [127]. It is notable (if not simply ironic) that

---

[12] Here we won't be addressing the related question whether tacit knowledge is a central characteristic of technology that distinguishes it from science [175, 54]. Albeit important, this question does not directly affect our task at hand. What's important for the purposes of this paper is the fact that technologies do produce accepted propositional knowledge.

the central historical example illustrating the third law in *The Laws of Scientific Change* is from medicine, which can be considered a field of technology. Specifically, the third law – the law of method employment – was illustrated by the case of multiple changes in drug testing methods: from a simple method of testing to the controlled trial method, then to the single-blind trial method, and finally to the double-blind trial method [4:p132-152].

By the third law, each one of these methods became employed at a certain point in time because it was a deductive consequence of respective accepted theories. Thus, once it was discovered that some unaccounted factors, such as the body's natural healing ability, improved nutrition, or improved climate, can affect a patient's health, we had to take this into consideration when testing drugs. The solution was the method of controlled trial, where two groups of patients participate in the trial: the *active* received the drug, while the control group was not given any drugs. If the improvement in the active group was greater than the improvement in the control group, the drug was said to be efficient. A similar transition in our expectations happened when we discovered the *placebo effect*, i.e. that the improvement in a medical condition can sometimes be due to the patient's belief that the treatment would improve their condition. This discovery altered our method of drug testing: the solution was to perform a *blind trial*, where the patients are unaware of which of the two groups they belong to. Thus, the patients in the control group would be given fake pills – placebos – but wouldn't know that the pills are fake. Finally, our drug testing methods were altered yet again when we discovered the phenomenon of *experimenter's bias*. Once we learned that the patients could be influenced by interaction with the researchers, we switched to the *double-blind* trial method, where neither the patients nor the researchers who are in contact with the patients know which group is which. If the improvement in the *active* group is greater than in the *placebo* group, we conclude that the drug is therapeutically effective.

This was arguably the central example used by Barseghyan to illustrate the third law of scientific change [4]. What it was meant to show is that changes in our expectations (i.e. our employed methods) are due to changes in our beliefs (i.e. our accepted theories). Importantly, we argue, it also shows that similar to scientific communities, technological communities also change their expectations as they learn new things about the world.

Our focus in this section will be on the second reason: the idea that scientific theories and methods are intrinsically intertwined with technological theories and methods. To appreciate this, consider a straightforward case of technology affecting method employment in science. Specifically, let's reflect on how our criteria of acceptance of astronomical observations have changed through time as we have learnt new things about both nature and artifacts.

Let us ask: what were the criteria of acceptance of the results of astronomical observations before the invention of the telescope in the early 1600s? Apparently, one tacit expectation of the astronomers during the period preceding the invention of the telescope was that astronomical data is to be obtained by means of naked-eye observations:

> Astronomical data is acceptable only if it is obtained in naked-eye observations.

It is safe to say that this was one of the implicit expectations towards astronomical data all the way until the late 16th century, i.e. the generation of Tycho Brahe [216]. Whether anyone in fact bothered to *openly* state these implicit expectations is beyond the point; what matters is that the actual expectations of the astronomers of the time were along these lines.[13] The invention of the telescope was followed by a period of heated debates on the trustworthiness of telescopic observations of celestial phenomena [58, 132]. However, it soon became accepted that telescopic observations can be a trustworthy source of astronomical data [84, 85]. In scientonomic terms, this was a change in the astronomers' expectations on what kind of observations can produce acceptable astronomical data. The acceptability of telescopic observations became part of their method:

> Astronomical data obtained by a telescope is acceptable.

There is nothing surprising about this change in the astronomer's method; that's exactly what is suggested by the third law: a new accepted theory shaped our methods of theory evaluation. In this case, the acceptance of the idea that telescopes can provide a trustworthy image of distant celestial objects led to changes in the astronomers' expectations concerning astronomical data.

---

[13] In scientonomy, there is an important distinction between the actual expectations of a community, i.e. their employed method, and their openly formulated methodological dicta [4:p52-61].

What is important for our current purposes is the fact that it was a new piece of *technological* knowledge that led to this change in the astronomers' method. Indeed, the proposition that telescopes make distant objects appear larger and closer is an instance of technological knowledge, as it concerns the workings of an artifact, the telescope. In other words, we have a case of a new accepted *technological* proposition shaping our method of acceptance of *scientific* theories. Here is the same idea in a typical scientonomic theory-method diagram:

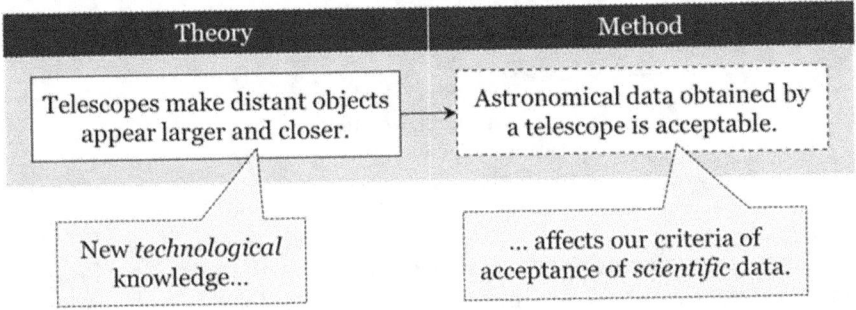

When we delve slightly deeper into the method of acceptance of astronomical observations employed in the 17th century, we notice another interesting phenomenon: scientific methods are often simultaneously affected by both *scientific* and *technological* beliefs. Consider the phenomenon of atmospheric refraction: once astronomers have learnt that light deviates when entering the atmosphere due to the varying densities of air in relation to heights, they began to take this into account and correct the measured positions of heavenly bodies accordingly [84]. Thus, a more precise explication of the method of acceptance of astronomical data employed at that time will be along these lines:

> Data obtained by a telescope is acceptable only if it the phenomenon of atmospheric refraction is accounted for.

From the scientonomic perspective, we have an instance of a method of evaluation of *scientific* propositions – in this case, a method of acceptance of astronomical data – which is being affected simultaneously by both accepted *technological* and accepted *scientific* theories – in this case, our belief in the trustworthiness of the telescope and our knowledge of atmospheric refraction:

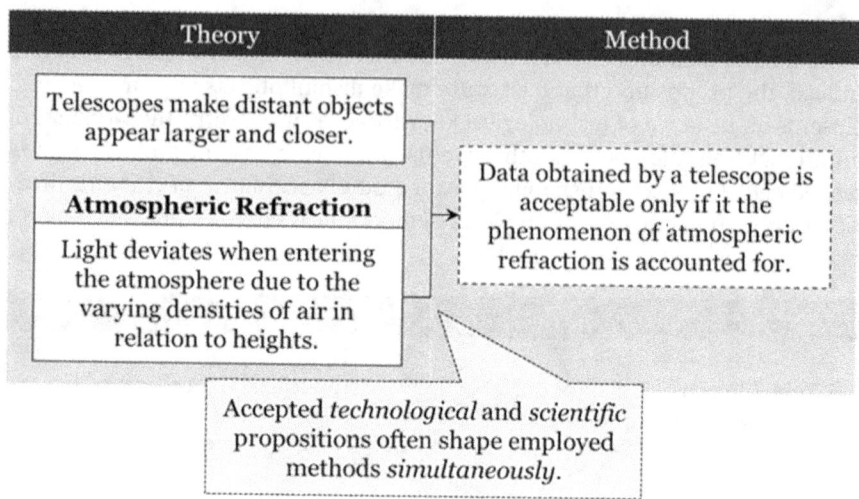

This finding is not surprising: one can cite a plethora of similar cases from our contemporary science, where methods of theory evaluation are customarily shaped *both* by our technological knowledge *and* by our scientific knowledge. Recall, for instance, the case of cell counting methods from *The Laws of Scientific Change*, where different technologies provided different implementations of the abstract requirement that, when counting the number of cells, the resulting value is acceptable only if it is obtained with an "aided" eye [4:p151-152]. What these examples show is that scientific and technological knowledge can be and often are intrinsically *intertwined*.

2.5 Concluding Remarks

We have argued that there *is* such a thing as accepted propositional technological knowledge and, importantly, that this accepted knowledge is intrinsically intertwined with accepted scientific theories and methods of their evaluation. First, technological theories and methods seem to exhibit the same *patterns* of change as theories and methods in natural, social, and formal sciences. In addition, accepted technological theories often *affect* the methods employed by communities in their evaluation of scientific theories.

Moreover, our preliminary research shows that, historically, a great majority of all accepted beliefs have been about the construction and operation of artifacts. This trivially holds for our contemporary mosaic, which contains great many accepted propositions from a wide range of technological fields (e.g. civil engineering, medicine, industrial biotechnology, nanotechnology, computer science, etc.). This also seems to hold for the mosaics of those communities that are traditionally considered less technology-oriented, such as any of the many versions of the Aristotelian-medieval mosaic accepted in the late medieval and early modern period. These mosaics contained not only accepted theories from natural philosophy, natural history, astronomy, theology etc., but also many propositions concerning such diverse technological subjects as agriculture, metallurgy, architecture, or navigation [86, 225].[14]

These findings suggest two interesting questions for future research. First, there is an important *historical* question: what were the different technological beliefs accepted by different epistemic communities at different times? Answering this question should become one of the major tasks of *the Tree of Knowledge* project and this data should be gradually added to the database of intellectual history. There is also an important *theoretical* question: what is the status and role of *inexplicable* (non-propositional) knowledge in the process of changes of theories and methods – technological or otherwise? The task is to find out whether there *is* such a thing and, if so, to understand how it changes through time.

---

[14] On earlier technology, see [226].

Chapter 3

Technology as an Aspect of Human Praxis

László Ropolyi

Eötvös Lóránd University

Summary

This paper proposes a specific approach to understanding the nature of technology that encompasses the entire field of technological praxis, from the making of primitive tools to using the Internet. In that approach, technology is a specific form of human agency that yields to (an imperfect) realization of human control over a technological situation—that is, a situation not governed to an end by natural constraints but by specific human aims. The components of such technological situations are a given collection of natural or artificial beings, humans, human aims, and situation-bound tools. By performing technological situation analysis, the essential form of tool making, the complex system of relationships between science and technology, technological practices with and without machines, the finiteness or imperfectness of any technology, and engineering (i.e., the possibility of the creation of technological situations) can be considered. For a better characterization of the approach to technology, the paper also presents a comparison of other philosophies of technology. Following Feenberg's comparative analysis, the so-called fundamental question of the philosophy of technology is formulated, its two sides are identified, and it is applied for clarification of our position within philosophy of technology. In our approach, all human praxis can be considered to be technological; more precisely, every human activity has a technological aspect or dimension.

3.1 Introduction

As to meet the objective of this paper, a rather special concept of technology is needed. In particular, the concept of technology must be broad enough to include technology in all its historical forms, primitive tool-making as well as recent information technologies. No doubt this is an "essentialist" view on technology since only an essentialist view is capable of accounting for the features that protean historical forms of technology have in common, and hence identifying the point in time when technology was born. However, instead of following in Heidegger's or Ellul's footsteps, I propose a different philosophy of technology based on a more universal concept of technology [183, 186, 184, 185].

I propose that the essence of technology is a specific form or aspect of human agency, the realization of the human control over a technological situation. In consequence of the deployment of this human agency, the course and the outcome of the situation are no longer governed by natural constraints but by specific human goals. The human control of technological situations yields artificial beings as outcomes. What is a technological situation? Technological situations are situations with a specific character. More concretely, technological situations vary and they are not homogeneous in nature, so, they can be identified on the basis of their constituents. The components that make up a technological situation are:

- a given set of (natural or artificial) beings,

- humans (human agencies),

- their aims, and

- (situation-bound) tools.

In Hegel's words, the essence of technology necessarily appears in concrete, particular technologies only, while on the other hand, all technologies necessarily embody the essence of technology. According to this view, every element of the human world is created by technologies. Even human nature and social being are the products of our technological activity, and their characteristics are determined by the specificities of the technologies we use to produce them.

In comparison with widely accepted views on technology, this view implies an extremely general and abstract conceptualization of technological praxis. In particular, all human praxis appears as technological, or better said, as having a technological aspect or dimension. The view on technology proposed above is therefore really close to a philosophy or theory of human practice. Human practice includes the—imperfect—realization of human control over a situation. Human practice is of course not identical with technological praxis, as the former has several other aspects as well, but it always and necessarily has a technological aspect too. Moreover, every human situation can be regarded as a technological situation, every human being as a technological agent, every human goal as accomplishable by a specific technology, and every human tool as a situation-bound technological tool. The technological aspect of human practice is a response to human vulnerability and expresses the intention to gain control over the situations of our lives. Without such an—evidently partial—success we would cease to be human beings; we would take part in natural situations as natural—animal—beings. For this reason, every technology is a technology of humanity: human beings, the human world, cultures and societies are all products of technologies. Further, technology is the only way humans can create themselves.

Human beings were born together with technologies – and technology was born together with human beings. Various branches of technology can be associated with various types of life situations. Our self-creating praxis is facilitated by a range of economic, legal, psychic, social, cultural, material, mechanical, etc. technologies.

In this view, engineering is a meta-technological activity, a specific practice of handling the components of technological situations, which aims to set up controllable situations in a given, complex, infinitely extending environment.

3.2 Philosophies of technology

For a better characterization of this approach to technology, a comparison of other philosophies of technology is needed. Of course, we cannot give a comprehensive overview of the philosophy of technology here; we are satisfied by recalling the approaches and problem areas which are closely connected to the general nature of technology. There are numerous books, journals and electronic sources of information for a more comprehensive review of the philosophy of technology.[1]

Most philosophers of technology agree with the claim according to which technology is a human product. People, following certain (according to different philosophers, different) aims operate technologies in order to satisfy basic human needs. According to the traditional view about humans and technology, technology is a complex tool and an act which make the forces of nature serve humans. As a result of technological activities, we intentionally transform the physical world to make it function according to our aims and to achieve a certain result. This means that we practically have a human or social control over technologies including their construction, use and developments. However, it is possible to conceive the work and even the emergence and change of technologies as autonomous processes of which are eventually not controlled or even not necessarily con-

---

[1] See e.g. [148, 149, 192, 42, 93, 95, 128, 47, 49, 160, 178]

trollable by particular human or social agents. All philosophies of technology include one of these (autonomous or controlled technology) positions.

All philosophies of technology take also a stand on the question of whether technology is value-neutral or value-laden. In other words, are the goals and means which are necessarily a part of technological activities separable from each other? If we assume their separability, given technological tools can successfully contribute to the realization of the most varied aims, that is, the tools themselves do not follow any goals, therefore in a certain sense they are neutral. Obviously, we can reach the same conclusion if we note that a given goal can be realized with different types of tools. In contrast, if we assume that tools have their own values, these are unavoidably built into the value system of the aim, since they will influence the goal that can be realized. That is, technology cannot be regarded as value-neutral but it is "value-laden" and we have to take its value content into account while using it.

Adopting Feenberg's chart [47, 50], a classification of the most significant versions of philosophies of technology based on the above-mentioned relations can be presented. Four main groups of classical philosophies of technology are differentiable: determinist, instrumentalist, substantivist, and critical versions. See in the Table (the table also contains some illustrative examples):

TECHNOLOGY	AUTONOMOUS	UNDER HUMAN CONTROL
VALUE NEUTRAL	*Determinism* Traditional Marxism	*Instrumentalism* Pragmatism
VALUE LADEN	*Substantivism* Anti-utopist views Ellul, Heidegger	*Critical theory* Anti-utopist views Marcuse, Foucault

The main characteristics of the philosophies of technology classified above can be identified on the basis of what we said earlier, but perhaps the choice of the names and the typical versions of the classes might require some explanation.

The *determinist* view has high hopes about the autonomous development of technology insofar as it regards technology as the key moving force of social progress. Technological progress is crucial in creating social progress, but the direction and the characteristics of social development are not determined by the values hidden in technology (since technology is value neutral), but by the goals chosen by people. A view such as this is in complete agreement with many versions of the modernist value system, for example, the modernist idea of clockwork or the traditional views of Marxism.

The *instrumentalist* view completely eliminates the connections between (technological) tools and (human) goals, for example, the idea that technological development necessarily generates social progress, and it interprets technological tools as means which can be freely utilized by man. The philosophical assumptions of instrumentalism are usually based on the ideas of liberalism or pragmatism [160].

Substantivism agrees with determinism in that humans are not the ruler of technology but rather is at the mercy of technological progress; what is more, according to this approach this is true in a very important sense. Technology is not neutral; it unavoidably expresses its own values during its usage, that is, technology necessarily modifies the goal to be reached and even modifies man himself. In this way, through enforcing the contents in themselves, technological tools shape the life of modern society as a determining factor (think of for example the effects of cars or television). Substantivist philosophy of technology (we could also say "factual", "essential" or "content based" as well) usually notes the negative social effects of technological progress and it often predicts anti-utopist scenarios. The emblematic figures of substantivism are Jacques Ellul [42] and the famous philosopher of the 20th century, Martin Heidegger. Heidegger's late writings are especially significant (written in the 50s and 60s) [82, 83, 96].

The characteristic figures of *critical philosophy of technology* (Mumford, Marcuse, Foucault, and Feenberg) developed their point of view under the influence of Heidegger and the Frankfurt School [47, 49, 51]. They accept the fact of the connection between the value content of technological tools and social aims. At the same time, they emphasize the possibility of human control over this interconnected conglomerate. In other words, though the technological and the human spheres are inseparably interconnected and this has numerous dangers, the unfolding processes can theoretically be handled through adequate political, economical or cultural means.

However, the question of the autonomy of technology is closely connected to the question of the value-neutral or value-laden nature of technology – in fact, they are different sides of the same relationship between technology and society. While during the interpretation of technology we paid attention to the circumstances which connect and separate technology and society, in connection with the value contents we examine a certain identity of technology and society and the possibilities of their appearance in each other. Obviously, both aspects have to be revealed for a successful description of the relationship between technology and society: their differences and their identity characterize their relationship appropriately together. The existence of such a fundamental question demands that every philosophy of technology has to declare its position in the relationship between technology and society. On the one hand, it is necessary to choose between the autonomous or non-autonomous (i.e., human-controlled) existence of technology; on the other, it is necessary to be for or against the value-laden nature of technology.

We can also express this by saying that the fundamental question of the philosophy of technology is the technology-society relationship, and it has two sides, namely the standpoints regarding the autonomy of technology and the value content of technology, which must both be found in any consistently constructed philosophy of technology – as it was demonstrated above.

3.3 Technology-society relation and human praxis

Let's consider the fundamental question of technology. First of all: how can we answer the fundamental question in our approach to technology?

1) *Human conditions as technological product.* As it is well known, Aristotle made a sharp distinction between natural and artificial beings (especially in his Physics). As he declared natural beings (they exist by nature) include in themselves the principles of motion and rest, but the artificial beings or artifacts (they exist from other causes) are products of the art of making things [87]. Based on this Aristotelian distinction the fundamental role of technologies – by definition as creators of the artificial spheres of beings – in the human world is really crucial.

Since human nature and social beings are artificial ones, technology is the only source of their emergence and existence. Every element of the human world is created by technologies. Both human nature and the social being are the products of our technological activity, and their characteristics are determined by the specificities of the technology we use to produce them. All historical forms of human nature and of social being are constructed (and continuously re-constructed) or produced (and continuously re-produced) by historical versions of technology. But technology has an ontological Janus face: it produces both "things" and "representations". For thousands of years, have people used material (agricultural or industrial) technologies where the material product was in the foreground, although the symbolic content was also present.

The last few decades have witnessed a significant technological change, in that "representations" have become dominant over the "thingly" products in the most important technologies of our age. On the one hand, new (cognitive, communication, cultural, and information) technologies have emerged; on the other hand, the representational or symbolic function of traditional technologies has become more significant. As a consequence, the most important characteristics of the social being are essentially transformed. The terms "post-industrial / knowledge / risk / information / network society" all refer to a type of society where representational technologies are the dominant factor in the (re)construction or the (re)production of human nature and of social being.

So, the technology as a specific form or aspect of human agency, as the realization of the human control over a technological situation is the fundamental creator of the human conditions.

2) *Technology as social product.* As it is well known social (or human) beings, obviously, can have an active, crucial role in the formation and functioning of any technology: given technological and social relations coexist and interrelate to each other in a complex way and the technological products and even the technology itself is a social product. There is no room to present any details here, in this way we just remind of the development of numerous versions of constructivist ideas on (science and) technology in the sociology of scientific knowledge (Mannheim, Bloor, Collins), in the social constructivism (Shapin and Schaffer), in the actor-network theory (Latour), in the phenomenological constructivism [7], in the radical constructivism [57], and so on. However, there can be found several interesting details in these disciplines on the social construction of technologies, but the most comprehensive and convincing view is the idea of the so-called social construction of technology (SCOT) proposed by Bijker and Pinch [155, 8] in which detailed descriptions and analyses are proposed on the constructive agents and mechanisms with several well-documented illustrations.

The SCOT emphasizes the crucial contributions of social actors to the formation of technologies, and the hermeneutics of science and technology (Ihde, Borgmann, Heelan) underline and disclose the human aspects of the constructive processes.

It is an essential aspect of the constructivist views, that engineering, obviously has a crucial – but in the different theories different – role in the process of construction. However, engineering in its traditional sense is not the only one actor of the construction. For example, in SCOT the "stabilization" of the features of an artifact happens in the course of a kind of discourse between engineers and different relevant social groups. In other words in this context there is a meaning to identify different kinds of "engineering", or the engineering has a heterogeneous character [107]. So, technologies are constructed by social (human) agents in a complex process of mutual actions.

3) *Technology-society interrelationships.* However, if the human conditions are technological products, and at the same time technologies are social (human) products, how can we avoid circular reasoning in the description of their causal relationships?

Let's take into account the fact, that this is not a really specific methodological dilemma, but the well-known difficulty of the understanding of complex systems, or the nature of complexity at all. Frankly, this difficulty can be considered as a (not irrelevant at all) definition of complexity, e.g. a complex system is a collection of a high number of interacting components with mutual determinations which can be explained with circular causality (see e.g. [45]). In other words, due to the appearance of circularity in the causal order, the technology-society conglomeration should have to be considered as a complex system.

However, it is very important that in the history of philosophy there have been emerged a very effective description of complexity: dialectics. Of course, the dialectical thinking, or dialectics as a methodology of thinking about complex beings, has been constructed in different versions with different efficiency. Hegel's dialectics in his Science of Logic can be considered as a genuine understanding of the world as totality – which is another name in philosophy for complexity. In our recent dilemma, a specific "application" of the Hegelian dialectical thinking will be used, which was performed by Marx in an unpublished manuscript thinking about the relationships between production and consumption [116]. In the chapter called "The General Relations of Production to Distribution, Exchange and Consumption" Marx clearly argues that the two crucial concepts, production and consumption stand in a very complex interrelationship. Here we have no possibility to reproduce the whole argumentation, but a kind of illustration of his dialectical thinking seems to be useful:

> *"Production is thus at the same time consumption, and consumption is at the same time production. Each is simultaneously its opposite. But an intermediary movement takes place between the two at the same time Each appears as a means of the other, as being induced by it; this is called their mutual dependence; they are thus brought into mutual relation and appear to be indispensable to each other, but nevertheless remain extrinsic to each other. Production is not only simultaneously consumption, and consumption simultaneously production; nor is production only a means of consumption and consumption the purpose of production but each of them by being carried through creates the other, it creates itself as the other."*

Marx additionally emphasizes that it would be necessary to avoid a kind of "empty Hegelianism" and based on these statements wrongly declaring that production and consumption are identical. The circular causation should be not the final statement. He continued the conceptual analysis involving additional relationships to seek out the more fundamental or the predominating factor of the production-consumption conglomeration in order to reach a real understanding of this complex being. According to our views, such kind of methodology can be successfully applied for a better understanding of any kind of complexity.

In this way, it seems to be possible to adopt this Marxian methodology in the case of a technology-society complex. Based on the above-mentioned relationships a kind of circular causation was disclosed in the technology-society complex. However, it seems to be necessary to go further and to find a really fundamental, predominant component in the complex. In our view, these are the human beings. As the first principle, the following is proposed: technologies are human technologies, societies are human societies. In other words: the active, acting human beings are situated in the center of the technology-society complex. The origins of this complex can be found at the human praxis.

So, to answer the fundamental question of the philosophy of technology we would propose not to use the separated concepts of autonomy and control, but instead of them the more sophisticated concept of technology-society complex seems to be relevant.

4) *Human praxis*. Human praxis (or practice) can be found at the origin of the technology-society complex. This means that all human praxis can be considered to be technological; more precisely, every human activity has a technological aspect or dimension. Human practice is not identical with technological praxis; it evidently has many another aspects, but every practice has a technological aspect.

Of course, philosophical considerations on human praxis have been an extended history with many consequences to the recent views on it. Here we attempt to limit ourselves to study only those aspects of the problem which are closely connected to the characterization of the specificity of our proposed philosophy of technology.

One of the most important philosophical problems is the understanding the "reification" in the context of human praxis.[2] Reification certainly is a fundamental component of the human praxis, but in our view that aspect which is not crucial in the understanding the technological aspect of the praxis. The "control over a situation" aspect of the praxis can be identified as a technological one.

There can be identified a kind of proliferation of conceptual tools applied in the description of praxis (or practice) in different philosophical traditions, so, speaking about human labor, social production, agency of actors, etc. we can refer similar conceptual structures in different contexts. The sophisticated translation of the terms and meanings to each other could be a topic of another study. Here we simply declare the aspiration that the proposed techno-

---

[2] An excellent discussion of these problems can be found in the book [2], especially in the papers [222, 103, 112, 106, 52].

logical interpretation of the praxis practically includes and refers to the common content of the different descriptions.

Every human practice yields to an – imperfect – realization of human control over a situation; i.e. the situation is not governed to an end by natural constraints but by specific human aims. Every human situation can be considered to be a technological one. Every human being is a technological agent. Every human aim is attainable by a specific technology. Every human tool can be considered to be a situation-bound technological tool.

The technological aspect of human practice embodies human defenselessness and human commitment to the successful control over the situations of human life. Without such obviously partial success, we would not survive as human beings but return to natural situations as natural – animal – beings. Every technology is a technology of humanity, and human beings, the human world, and human cultures and societies are equally products of technologies. Technology is the only tool for human self-creation. The branches of technologies can be associated with families of life situations. Different economic, legal, psychical, social, cultural, material, and mechanical technologies serve humans' self-creating praxis. In that sense, different kinds of engineering can be considered to be a meta-technological activity at different situations: a specific practice of handling the components of the given technological situations with the aim of cultivating controllable situations in the human environment.

Notice that in this philosophy of technology the concept of situation has a central role. A situation is a (finite or infinite) collection or set of beings which includes, as an element, at least a human being. Every situation is a human situation. The concept of situation is closely related to the concept of world and the concept of system. Every world includes at least a human being, so the worlds are human worlds, similarly as it was declared in the case of situations, but the world is an organized totality around the humans, in contrast to the situation of which has no such a structure. From a structural point of view, the situation is similar to the systems. A system is a set of beings taking arbitrarily together without any given structure. However the situation is given, the system is freely chosen. So, the situation can be considered as a world without structure or a system without constitutive freedom.

Let's repeat the characterization of the technological situation. Technological situations are situations with a specific character. More concretely, technological situations vary and they are not homogeneous in nature, so, they can be identified on the basis of their constituents. The components that make up a technological situation are:

- a given set of (natural or artificial) beings,
- humans (human agencies),
- their aims, and
- (situation-bound) tools.

Based on the above comparative notes we can speak about technological systems, but it is impossible to aspire to the control over the world. In practice, the human world is disjointed into controllable situations.

For the connection of these ideas to Heidegger famous analyzes in his paper "The Question Concerning Technology", we can consistently substitute Heidegger's concept of "Gestell" (Enframing) for the concept of "technological situation" used above. In this case, perhaps we will also notice that our standpoint in the characterization of the historical forms of technology is significantly different from Heidegger's. According to Heidegger, there is a sharp difference between Ancient and modern technology (the earlier is creative, the latter is related to power). However, we believe that this differentiation is unjustified: creation and power can only characterize any kind of technology together [83].

So, in this view of technology, the fundamental question of philosophy of technology can be answered considering the technology-society complex in the context of human praxis. Technology and society coexisting and their complex is value-laden. This view of technology can be considered as a version of critical philosophy of technology.

3.4 Perspectives on the science-technology relationships

The inseparability of technological and human spheres, that is, the human values built into technological tools as well as imagining technological tools which influence human aims, have become more or less completely accepted in the endeavors of the philosophy of technology. Thus, in fact, we can say that the popular views of the philosophy of technology nowadays are either substantivist or critical philosophies of technology or a certain mixture of these. Nevertheless, they might diverge in several details. For example, if we compare the views of contemporary philosophers of technology such as Pickering, Haraway, Latour or Ihde [92], it becomes clear that the analysis of the problematic relationship between the human and the non-human is centrally important for all of them (though they use different concepts). Thus, for example, they characteristically make a stand in connection with the possibly symmetric nature of the relationship between the human and the non-human, the nature of the activity of technological tools, the possibility of the incarnation of human intentions in non-human entities and the incarnation of non-human strivings in humans and in similar connected questions.

Notice, that the dominance of the philosophical ideas of hermeneutics, social constructivism and the postmodern point of view in the philosophy of technology is basically connected to the nature of technology. As was already discussed, technology can always be interpreted in a certain situation, that is, it is a situation-dependent entity. Entities and forms of existence of this kind are difficult to interpret for philosophical systems such as positivism or the whole tradition of analytic philosophy since these points of view precisely concentrate on researching and describing entities and knowledge which are situation-independent. However, hermeneutics, the postmodern approach, and social constructivism precisely deal with the interpretation of entities and forms of existence embedded in a situation (world, life-world, social environment), that is, as a result of their basic philosophical assumptions, they are more appropriate for describing and interpreting situation-dependent technology. Consequently, we can also say that hermeneutics, social constructivism, and postmodern philosophical systems are systems of the philosophy of technology as well since they necessarily include the possibility of interpreting technology philosophically, though of course only in an implicit form, or using a Hegelian term, in an unhappy form.

We can utilize the mentioned philosophical points of view not only for interpreting technology but also in the interpretation and description of the sciences. In fact, it is our experience that hermeneutical, social constructivist, feminist, etc. points of view have also developed in the philosophy of science. In these philosophies of science, they try to understand science (either the whole of science or some of its problems) by placing it into some kind of (human or social) situation. The consequence of this is that the methodology of interpreting technology and science is necessarily identical in the mentioned approaches. As a result of the identical points of view, the differences between technology and science might be blurred or might seem insignificant since we understand all of them chiefly as a certain being-in-the-world, as something which fits into a context. In recent years, the outlines of an independent entity called technoscience have been developing from the common characteristics of technology and science which we identified with the situation-dependent point of view described above. The interpretation of technoscience is more and more popular worldwide, and it is gradually taking over the roles of "traditional" philosophy of technology and philosophy of science which were earlier regarded as separate [154], [92].

Given the above conceptualization of technology, it is evident that technology has primacy over intellectual practices such as doing philosophy or doing science. This is because being a human is prerequisite for being a philosopher or for being a scientist. Evidently, there is no philosophy or science without specific, historically determined technological practices. In other words: philosophy and science (as well as any other field of human culture) necessarily rely on and thus include technological components [185]. The fundamental interrelations of science, philosophy and technology can be summarized in a schematic formula: "science = technology + philosophy" [182].

Part II -
Post-Critical Philosophy of Technology

Chapter 4

Essays on Post-Critical Philosophy of Technology

Eszter Nádasi

One of the main figures of the so-called "post-critical genre of philosophy" is Michael Polanyi. This component of the book introduces some of the main philosophical views of the Hungarian-British polymath, by focusing on his ideas that are connected to engineering and machines.

For an overview of what post-critical means, it is worth citing the definition from the study of Mihály Héder:

> "The phrase 'post-critical' in the subtitle summarizes the main statement very well. That is: while the critical, objectivist approach – Polanyi uses these terms broadly to portray all approaches that attempt to remove the personal coefficient from knowing – in epistemology has been a tremendously useful for humanity, it only succeeded because it has never been exercised in a perfectly systematic manner, leaving room for uncritical elements in the production of knowledge"

Héder's essay, entitled *Michael Polanyi and the Epistemology of Engineering*, reviews Polanyi's magnum opus *Personal Knowledge*. The author collects a broad set of philosophical ideas that he sees as relevant to engineering from Polanyi's book. His central claim is although Polanyi is not seen as a figure primarily engaged in the philosophy of technology, his overarching theory yields a consistent philosophy of technology. This includes ontological claims about the nature of machines and the operational principles they embody. He also explains Polanyi's notion of dual control which refers to the cooperation of laws of nature and ordering principles in all machines and living things. Heder also reflects on the epistemological part of engineering, especially the heuristic passions that drive the work of the inventor towards a heuristic act of contrivance. Finally, Héder argues for placing tacit knowledge on the map of engineering epistemology, raising the possibility of its importance for basic engineering research.

The second study of Part II, written by Phil Mullins deals with the nature of machines. Mullins does this in the context of all Polanyi's writings, which he comprehensively reviews. He focuses on the concept of the "comprehensive entity", which Polanyi started using in the middle period of his philosophical development:

> "In writing after the publication of PK, "comprehensive entity" becomes a more frequently and broadly used term for Polanyi. Although sometimes he applies the term to "comprehensive biotic entities" and machines, he later seems to use the term more generically to mean any object of knowledge or focus of attention for a skillful knower."

Mullins presents a detailed explanation of the evolution of this term in the context of the overall development of Polanyi's thinking. He investigates the extent to which this term is an ontological one. Also, he explains Polanyi's use of the term to characterized living things as well as to machines; he also outlines the Polanyian ideas about digital computers. At the end, Mullins moves beyond the statements of Polanyi and contemplates the question about artificial intelligence which contemporary learning machines in particular raise. He thereby connects his work with the fascinating and very recent applications of artificial intelligence, including prediction systems used by a Pittsburgh children's welfare office, recent breakthroughs in deep neural networks, and voice recognition systems such as Siri and Alexa.

The importance of Michael Polanyi's work in the field of post-critical philosophy of technology inspired the editors to select the title *Essays in Post-Critical and Contemporary Philosophy of Technology* for the whole book.

Chapter 5

Michael Polanyi on Machines as Comprehensive Entities

Phil Mullins

Missouri Western State University

Summary

This essay analyzes Michael Polanyi's ideas about what he calls a "comprehensive entity." It focuses on the way Polanyi compares and contrasts living beings and machines as "comprehensive entities." In particular, I examine Polanyi's mid-century account of computers as machines and suggest that contemporary deep learning neural networks operating in digital culture suggest some of Polanyi's thinking needs to be recast.

Acknowledgement: This chapter was supported by the János Bolyai Research Scholarship of the Hungarian Academy of Sciences.

5.1 Introduction

This essay extends my earlier efforts to sort out Michael Polanyi's rich and provocative philosophical ideas about what he calls "comprehensive entities." His discussions suggest that living beings are one kind of "comprehensive entity" and machines are another and he illumines the nature of these two types of entities by comparing and contrasting living beings and machines. Although I begin by summarizing and re-framing some of my earlier conclusions [140, 136, 137], I primarily intend here to analyze Polanyi's discussion of machines in order to raise questions relevant to the philosophy of technology. I provide some background on Polanyi's use of the term "comprehensive entity," and then turn to some of his claims about comprehensive entities and finally to some broader questions about contemporary machines.

5.2 The History of Polanyi's Use of "Comprehensive Entity"

"Comprehensive entity" is a term Polanyi begins to use in the middle period of his philosophical development (roughly 1950-1958), and he uses the term sparingly and quite concretely at first. But in his late writing after *Personal Knowledge* ([175], hereafter PK), he uses the term more frequently and more generically than earlier.[1]

I have found only one instance of the use of "comprehensive entity" in Polanyi's Gifford Lectures given in 1951 and 1952 [161]. That occurs in his eighth Series II lecture (1952) titled "Living Beings."[2] Here he notes simply that, when considering a number of varied specimens of a species, there is a "merging of specimens into a comprehensive entity" and this is a process of "merging molecular facts into a molar entity by an act of personal judgment" (15). In the six years after his Gifford Lectures, Polanyi worked diligently with Marjorie Grene to revise his Gifford Lectures to produce PK (PK, xv). However, the term "comprehensive entity" is also used sparingly in PK. "Comprehensive entity" is not listed in the PK Index, but there are more than ten entries (some with multiple page references) for "comprehension" (PK, 411). Clearly, this is Polanyi's main interest, as I discuss below. Although Polanyi does use "comprehensive entity" early in PK, (e.g., PK, 64), most of the uses of the term appear in the final section of the book, the "Knowing and Being" section of the text (PK, 327-405), the last three chapters (paralleling and expanding the final three Series II Gifford Lectures) in which discussion moves from the more general problem of knowing to the matter of knowing living beings and the evolution of living beings. Evolution includes, in Polanyi's account, preeminently the emergence of human beings with an enormous range of tacit powers that can, in fact, be deployed in thoughtful inquiry about living beings and the larger cosmos in which all life is situated.

"Comprehensive entity" is thus a term Polanyi used in PK primarily to designate known living beings, as Marjorie Grene notes in *The Knower and the Known* ([67, 223-224], hereafter KK). He discusses the "three-storied knowing" in biology (PK, 364). To study a simple amoeba, Polanyi argues, requires recognizing a "comprehensive entity" which is active in an environment, but so also does the

---

[1] References to *Personal Knowledge* are to the Harper Torchbook edition (Harper & Rowe, New York, NY, 1964) which includes the important "Preface to the Torchbook Edition."
[2] Polanyi's Series I and II Gifford Lectures are online at http://www.polanyisociety.org/Giffords/Giffords-web-page9-20-16.htm (accessed December 4, 2017). On the same page, there is a link for my essay "An Introduction to Michael Polanyi's Gifford Lectures" and "Syllabus For Series I." Individual Gifford Lectures as well as these other materials are cited by page below. Citations from online material are handled in the text where feasible.

study of the much more biologically complex, language using, culturally embedded human being who interprets and responds to her world in complex ways. Sometimes (although not consistently) Polanyi uses the more specific term "comprehensive biotic entity" (PK, 432) to distinguish living beings as members of the broader class of "comprehensive entities." Interestingly and importantly, Polanyi's discussion also (in PK and later writing) carefully applies the term "comprehensive entity" to machines (see the discussion below). To study any "comprehensive entity" requires a preliminary grasping of a Gestalt (a molar view). Following up on suggestions in his earlier Gifford Lecture discussion, Polanyi contends that recognizing the difference between a "molar" and a "molecular" perspective is important (PK, 327-332).[3]

In writing after the publication of PK, "comprehensive entity" becomes a more frequently and broadly used term for Polanyi. Although sometimes he applies the term to "comprehensive biotic entities" and machines, he later seems to use the term more generically to mean any object of knowledge or focus of attention for a skillful knower. Such focal attention recognizes a coherence by integrating subsidiarily known particulars; a "comprehensive entity" comprehends or includes such subsidiary particulars, but it does so in a way that reflects their bearing on the focal or distal whole's meaning. Earlier in PK, Polanyi also discussed the integration of subsidiaries, but he does not so frequently designate the integrated whole a "comprehensive entity" unless he is referring to compre-

---

[3] As some of the discussion below points out, Polanyi after PK has more to say about coherences and their relative degree of "reality," which is concerned with the realization of signifying potential. In his 1966 book *The Tacit Dimension* ([173], hereafter TD), he says "the capacity of a thing to reveal itself in unexpected ways in the future I attribute to the fact that the thing observed is an aspect of a reality, possessing a significance that is not exhausted by our conception of any single aspect of it"(TD, 32). As Grene notes in KK, Polanyi is not opting for an idealist view that absorbs all extension into intension. Nor is he arguing for a "fixed, universal hierarchy which the recognition of degrees and dimensions of being seeks to restore" (KK, 223). Even more importantly, he is not arguing that "sheer givenness" is "the only way things are" (KK, 223). But Polanyi is suggesting that "knowledge itself" is "a real achievement of real beings" (KK, 223). "Comprehensive entity" becomes the term, in my view, that Polanyi primarily uses to make his case. Mihály Héder, in "Michael Polanyi and the Epistemology of Engineering," [80] suggests Polanyi articulates a scale of the relative intensity of coherences running from the simple to complex living beings. Perhaps there are hints of this scale in Polanyi's writing suggested by his interest in randomness, ordering principles and operational principles. Nevertheless, I find Polanyi's emphasis upon relative degrees of reality primarily a metaphysical move concerned with the recovery of meaning and the responsible human calling to vocations of inquiry as well as other callings. Polanyi points to recovery of a hierarchical account of the universe as a way for human beings to again become at home in the universe.

hending a living being. But his more general use of the term can be found in The *Study of Man* ([164], hereafter SM; e.g., SM, 44, 45, 46, 65, 66) published soon after PK in 1959, as well as in several of Polanyi's lectures series given in the sixties such as the 1964 Duke Lectures [167].

In my view, Polanyi does not seem to have sorted out all of the metaphysical issues connected with his more generic use of "comprehensive entity." At least some "comprehensive entities" such as human minds and good problems, Polanyi regards as coherences which should be recognized as having a dynamic depth which he suggests is a future revelatory potential or power; he regards such coherences as profoundly real "comprehensive entities" and perhaps all such profoundly real coherences should be regarded as having emergent dimensions. Polanyi sometimes does, as he does in the case of emergent comprehensive biotic entities, focus on the relation between levels in non-biotic comprehensive entities such as machines (e.g., SM, 46-47). But his discussion of machines, unlike that of minds, good problems and, evolving comprehensive biotic entities does not emphasize the emergence of new levels. Sometimes Polanyi implies that we can distinguish "epistemic emergents" (i.e., richly real entities with indeterminate future manifestations—my term) from comprehensive biotic entities that emerge in evolutionary history, but all comprehensive entities are for Polanyi skillfully known realities. I am wary of making too much of a distinction between "epistemically emergent" entities and comprehensive biotic entities that are emergent insofar as this seems a distinction that quickly slides into presuppositions about mind and matter, and it seems wrongly to imply that Polanyi's account of comprehensive entities gives priority to mind-independent entities. Both good problems and comprehensive biotic entities seem to be historically emergent phenomena, although the time scale is vastly different for biological emergence. Polanyi seems to presuppose that all comprehensive entities that are emergent entities must be regarded as embedded in an ongoing tradition of inquiry in one or another community of interpretation; future inquirers in a particular community of interpretation may discover aspects of richly real emergent entities that are not presently recognized. This is the case with both comprehensive biotic entities and non-biotic comprehensive entities.

The history of Polanyi's changing use of "comprehensive entity" should be understood in terms of the broader development of his thinking. The early phase in the development of Polanyi's "post-critical" account of understanding is articulated in his Gifford Lecture and PK and is focused on what Polanyi called the "fiduciary program" (PK, 264-268) which emphasized the centrality of belief. This is the phase in which "comprehensive entity" is used in Part IV of PK primarily to refer to knowing living beings. The succeeding phase of the development of Polanyi's post-critical account of understanding is an extension and refinement of ideas in the fiduciary program as Polanyi works out his epistemological model identified as the operation of "tacit knowing" (PK, ix-xi, 164-169).[4] In the next decade after the publication of PK, Polanyi works out an epistemological model which he called "tacit knowing" that focuses on the "from-to" structure of all knowing (TD, x) and (in an essay of the same title) the "logic of tacit thought" [172]. In the sixties, Polanyi's efforts to discuss the active nature of comprehension in the theory of tacit knowing focuses in on what he calls the functional and phenomenal structure of tacit knowing and the semantic and ontological aspects of tacit knowing.

5.3 The Bodily and Polyvalent Dimensions of "Comprehensive Entities"

Whether Polanyi uses "comprehensive entity" primarily to refer to living beings and machines (as in PK) or, more generally, to point to any comprehensive integration of subsidiaries, Polanyi's term emphasizes the active and personal participation of the knower in the known. His constructive philosophical objective from the time of his 1951-52 Gifford Lectures was to re-frame the mainstream understanding of understanding. Polanyi recognized that he was turning Gestalt ideas into an epistemology and this effort was one that emphasized the importance of the spontaneous, the indeterminate and the non-explicit (PK, xiii).

Knowing for Polanyi is primarily a species of action of the human comprehensive entity. Other animals and perhaps other living creatures also participate in a particular lifeworld in a way analogous to human knowing—they too are actors— but this is a complicated matter that Polanyi seems only partially to have addressed. He does, however, generally suggest that the development and use of tacit powers in the evolutionary history of comprehensive biotic entities is the best way to understand living agency.

In the human case of knowing, neither the knower nor the known can be analyzed in strict independence and accounts which insistently separate them are a dangerous cul-de-sac. Such accounts led to the dominant mid-twentieth century tendency to proclaim that legitimate explanations must focus on the least parts. As I have noted, the Index of PK suggests Polanyi's primary interest is in the process of comprehension of a living human agent. His account of comprehension is an account that steadfastly avoids any sort of preliminarily presupposed ontological separation of the knower and the

---

[4] In PK there are ideas about tacit knowing. These citations, however, do point to places Polanyi, as well as Grene, noted development in Polanyi's thought over the course of his years doing philosophical writing. Below I also discuss Polanyi comment in a 1966 interview [171] which also describes what he regarded as a new development in his thinking in 1962.

known, as is found in the early modern Descartes' *res extensa* and *res cogitans*, as well as the medieval nominalist disposition to locate the real as first and foremost in mind-independent existents (a supposition that carries forth in Descartes and later thinkers).

Polanyi emphasizes that the knower and known are inextricably and relationally bound together; he does this by simultaneously emphasizing both the bodily and the polyvalent dimensions of comprehensive entities.[5] Comprehensive entities have a bodily dimension insofar as those who grasp such entities must dwell in subsidiaries and actively shape or coordinate their tacit integration. The bodily dimension of comprehension and comprehensive entities is also emphasized (although a little differently) in existential phenomenology insofar as Being-in-the-world is a primary theme. Living human beings (and Polanyi implies this is the case for all living beings) are always already embodied in a particular niche that is itself changing. Living beings extend themselves into that niche—they indwell–and their agency is bound up with a particular niche (at a particular time) and the ways active indwelling and integration work to realize certain affordances. Polanyi (with some help from Marjorie Grene) eventually understood the link between his philosophical perspective emphasizing tacit knowing and that of figures like Heidegger and Merleau-Ponty.

Polanyi not only emphasizes the bodily dimension of comprehensive entities but he also emphasizes that comprehensive entities have a polyvalent dimension insofar as such entities open up the indeterminate meaning of reality.[6] Polanyi is interested in the growth of meaning through individual

---

[5] "Bodily" and "polyvalent" are terms I have used to capture the two dimensions of Polanyi's participative realism. See my discussion in [137, 16-21] and [136, 42-50]. Polanyi himself has much to say about the "bodily" nature of subsidiaries so this is likely not a strange term to those familiar with Polanyi. But "polyvalent" is a term used in literary theory rather than one of Polanyi's terms. "Polyvalence" is concerned with the rich meaning potential of coherences. Polanyi is a thinker interested in the growth of meaning and his comments about those coherences that are most real are concerned with the resonant depth of significance of such coherences. Such richly real coherences are "polyvalent" and this designation has an anticipatory and public nuance overlooked by metaphysical accounts of the "real" which give priority to matters of existence.

[6] Polanyi connects polyvalence with vagueness in his 1966 essay "The Logic of Tacit Inference" (Polanyi, 1966b, included in the collection of Polanyi essays *Knowing and Being* edited by Marjorie Grene [listed in References as [69] but cited hereafter as KB by page number): "The vagueness of something like the human mind is due to the vastness of its resources. Man can take in at a glance any one of 1040 different sentences. By my definition, this indeterminacy makes mind the more real, the more substantial" (KB,151). Po-

human action and through the action of communities of interpretation such as science in which individuals participate in an ongoing public conversation about their projects of inquiry which explore the nature of the real. Polanyi suggests that inquiry is the special human vocation; human beings have gifts—extraordinary tacit powers which have emerged in evolutionary history, which in the human case is also a historical-cultural journey—that allow us responsibly to study biology and ultrabiology and indeed the whole cosmos. Polanyi emphasizes the growth of thought in a society of explorers. Scientific discovery is at the center of his interest, although he carefully links scientists' work toward discoveries to the efforts to cope and flourish of all comprehensive biotic entities. The polyvalent dimension of comprehensive entities fits with the calling of the biocultural human comprehensive entity whose special vocation is inquiry. Responsible inquiry is a kind of human action Polanyi believes will allow humans to better understand the natural order in which we belong and make us at home in the world.

5.4 Polanyi's Use of Ontological Language

In his writing in the sixties, Polanyi does at least for a few years adopt ontological language to describe comprehensive entities.[7] But he is very careful in

---

lanyi thus recognized the vagueness of complex real things and indicated that such vagueness is not merely a matter of language understood as a set of convenient and conventional symbols. Polanyi was quite critical of what he regarded as the nominalistic underpinnings of most philosophical views of language at mid-century. He criticized views emphasizing the "open texture" of terms, claiming it is necessary to accredit a "speaker's sense of fitness for judging that his words express the reality he seeks to express" (PK, 114).

[7] Meek, in the revised and expanded version of her dissertation from the mid-eighties [120, 91 n.12], reports that Grene advised her that Polanyi became disenchanted with ontological language and regretted using it in some of his writing. She points out (2017, 89-96) that Polanyi used ontological language only for a few years in the sixties in some lectures, essays and books but not in others; she argues Polanyi seems to understand the "ontological aspect" in two different ways that are in tension. What Grene reports is of interest and Polanyi's use of ontological language is limited, but it is careful and grows out of his developing interest in the "comprehensive entity" and his effort to move from his fiduciary program toward his more refined theory of tacit knowing. Meek does not seem to appreciate Polanyi's early account of levels in Part IV of PK and the way this account is developed further after 1962. She plays off against each other what she sees as Polanyi's two senses of the ontological aspect, one concerned with levels and the parallel structure of knowing and being, and the other concerned with authentic contact with reality which produces indeterminate future manifestations. Her interest is primarily in Polanyi's focus on contact with reality and the indeterminate future manifestations of such contact and she thinks Polanyi abandoned his interest in what

what he says about ontology. His move to ontological language is a component of his effort, noted above, to describe the active nature of comprehension in a more refined epistemological model. He hones in on what he calls the functional and phenomenal structure of tacit knowing and the semantic and ontological aspects of tacit knowing.

Polanyi's interest, in the sixties, in carefully introducing ideas about the ontological dimension of tacit knowing is an outgrowth of working out more clearly his ideas about marginal or boundary control. In an unpublished 1966 interview with Ray Wilken,[8] Polanyi claimed that in his 1962 essay "Tacit Knowing: Its Bearing on Some Problems in Philosophy" [166], he reinforced his relatively weak critique of mechanism provided in PK (probably he had in mind PK, 328-331, 343-346, and 381-382) and added a new argument ("the most decisive things which have come out since Personal Knowledge"). In this interview, he suggests that in PK he argued machines could not be represented in terms of physics and chemistry and this was a case based on his claims about molar recognition.[9] But he later developed the stronger argument that levels of reality in comprehensive entities are irreducible because of the "principle of boundary control" which shows the structure in comprehensive entities through which such entities exist: thus "the same system can be under two or three or four or five fold control of different principles be-

---

she calls the parallel structure. Meek's emphasis upon contact with reality and the indeterminate future manifestations of reality is akin to what I have above (and elsewhere in [140]) noted as the polyvalent dimension of comprehensive entities. My approach, summarized in this essay, takes Polanyi's effort to expand his ideas about "comprehensive entities" as an important metaphysical extension of his thought whose implications Polanyi works out more fully over several years. Polanyi outlines a metaphysical element that is decidedly anti-Cartesian and realist in Polanyi's peculiar sense.

[8] Interviews of Polanyi by Ray Wilken (April 5 and 6, 1966), Wesleyan Interview Transcript 3 File, pp. 9-10 at http://www.polanyisociety.org/WilkenInterview/WslynIntrvwApr5&6-1966-transcript-file3.pdf (accessed December 30, 2017) from which I quote in this paragraph (listed in References as Polanyi, 1966a).

[9] The Wilken interview suggests that the Part IV argument in PK Polanyi came to regard as having focused on the irreducibility of conceptions while his post-PK argument (perhaps beginning with his 1962 essay) shows "how such structures can exist. This is the principle of boundary control." See the discussion following. Polanyi clearly seems to be claiming that his PK criticism of mechanism and reducibility paid attention primarily to the nature of conceptions, but he later "reinforced" this with a "new argument" that pays attention to "levels of reality" (transcript-file 3, p. 10). As I suggest at the end of this paragraph, Polanyi new insight seems to be a prerequisite for his discussions of the "ontological" aspect of tacit knowing and comprehensive entities, which appears in his writing beginning in the early sixties.

cause each stratum has its boundaries controlled by another higher principle; and the case of the machine is now analyzed and properly established in these terms." In sum, Polanyi's deeper understanding of the way in which "boundary conditions" are "governed" in machines and living forms is a prerequisite for his discussion of the "ontological aspect" as a generalization applying to all comprehensive entities; this extension is a move beyond the argument in Part IV, "Knowing and Being," of PK.

In *The Tacit Dimension*, which was published in 1966 but based on his 1962 Terry Lectures, Polanyi discusses how tacit knowing makes an "*ontological* reference" (TD, 33) to comprehensive entities. He argues that comprehensive entities include skillful performances such as conducting a game of chess (TD, 40); all comprehensive entities are thus more or less skillful activities (and are thus grounded in a complementary hierarchy of habituated skills).[10] Such activity Polanyi says is "similar in structure to that which it comprehends" (TD, 40) so that an "*ontological* reference" identifies what we grasp or understand in the activity which is the entity or performance. In the opening chapter of TD ("Tacit Knowing"), Polanyi affirms that the "*ontological* aspect" (TD, 13) of tacit knowing is an inference drawn from the other three aspects of tacit knowing: "From the three aspects of tacit knowing that I have defined so far—the functional, the phenomenal, and the semantic—we can deduce a fourth aspect which tells us what tacit knowing is a knowledge of. This will represent its *ontological* aspect" (TD, 13).[11]

In the fourth Duke Lecture (1964), Polanyi again sets forth his ideas about the ontological dimension or aspect of all comprehensive entities but this statement is clearer insofar as he omits possibly misleading language about "correspondence" used in TD (33-34). He emphasizes that skillful human performances are comprehensive entities and stresses that such performances are real things which are "as real as cobblestones and, in view of their far greater independence and power, much **more** real than cobblestones (Duke,

---

[10] "Knowledge is an activity which would be better described as a process of knowing." (KB,132). This clear affirmation comes in Polanyi's 1961 essay "Knowing and Being," ([165], included in KB) which is the year before the 1962 Terry Lectures.

[11] Polanyi apparently chose to call the ontological aspect a "deduction" (a term used only in TD so far as I can determine) from the other aspects of tacit knowing because a deduction is the strongest type of logical inference. The "ontological aspect" is a non-amplicative conclusion about the nature of a comprehensive entity which follows, given an integrative performance which can be described in terms of the functional and the phenomenal structure, and the semantic aspect.

IV-5).¹² Since this is the case, it is reasonable to regard all other instances of tacit knowing as cases in which

> "the structure of that which it comprehends and to go further and expect **to find the structure of tacit knowing duplicated in the principles which account for the stability and effectiveness of all real comprehensive entities**" (Duke, IV-5).

Here, as in TD, Polanyi emphasizes the "plausibility" of a generalization covering all cases of tacit knowing, which is the process through which we understand "all real comprehensive entities." This generalization focuses on the operation of principles at different levels, which provides "stability and effectiveness of all real comprehensive entities."

In the discussion of "The Creative Imagination," an address drafted in early 1965 and delivered as the opening keynote at the August, 1965 Bowdoin College meeting of the Study Group for Cultural Unity, Polanyi suggested the relationship between the functional, phenomenal and semantic aspects of tacit knowing defines a reality, and this is "the ontological aspect of tacit relations."¹³ In his 1966 essay "The Logic of Tacit Inference" (an essay is based on a paper first presented in Jerusalem soon after his spring 1964 Duke Lectures),

---

[12] All five Duke Lectures and my introduction are available online at http://www.polanyisociety.org/Duke-intro.htm (accessed December 30, 2017). At the beginning of the fifth and final Duke Lecture, Polanyi summarizes his preceding lecture, suggesting it made clear how the structure of tacit knowing is duplicated in the structure of a comprehensive entity. His analysis of the way tacit knowing works in human performances showed that *"what* is comprehended has the same structure as the act that comprehends it. The relation of a comprehensive entity to its particulars was then generally recognized as the relation between two levels of reality, the higher one controlling the marginal conditions left indeterminate by the principles governing the lower one." Levels can be stacked to form a hierarchy and this suggests a stratified universe: "Stratification offered a framework for defining emergence as the action which produces a higher level, first from the inanimate to the living and then from each biotic level to the one above it. Emergence would operate in this way both in the development of an individual and in the evolution of living beings" (Duke, V-1).

[13] The discussion of Polanyi's address in which Polanyi makes this comment is in the Grene-edited monograph *Toward A Unity of Knowledge* [70, 73-74] with 1965 conference materials. "The Creative Imagination" in a slightly varied form is the third of the Fall, 1965 Wesleyan Lectures ([170] online at http://www.polanyisociety.org/WesleyanLectures/WesleyanLecturesIntro.htm [accessed January 10, 2018]) and was published in several other places as well as in Grene's monograph.

Polanyi says tacit integration presents a "real coherent entity" and such an entity "embodies the *ontological claim* of tacit knowing. The act of tacit knowing thus implies the claim that its result is an aspect of reality which, as such, may yet reveal its truth in an inexhaustible range of unknown and perhaps still unthinkable ways."(KB, 141).[14] In sum, these several instances of Polanyi's account of ontology reflect Polanyi's commitment to what I have called both the bodily and polyvalent dimensions of tacit knowing. Marjorie Grene nicely summarized what is Polanyi's approach to ontology when she commented in *The Knower and the Known* (a book which incorporated material from Polanyi's Duke Lectures) what philosophy needed is "a frankly epistemological approach to metaphysics to set right the epistemological errors of Descartes with which modern philosophy began" (KK, 244).

5.5 On Comprehending Living Things and Machines

Polanyi compares and contrasts comprehensive biotic entities and machines as comprehensive entities and this serves as a way to illumine both kinds of comprehensive entities. This analogical link first appears in PK and is focused around matters concerned with the problem of understanding both types of comprehensive entities. Polanyi argues that comprehension of both living beings and machines acknowledges a molar achievement which cannot be specified in molecular terms.

Polanyi contended that scientists in his era often misunderstood machines since they held that it is possible to analyze and understand the success of machines in terms of physics and chemistry. He suggests that this view is the outgrowth of an inclination toward reductionism in contemporary science, an inclination that he argues has not had an altogether negative influence on science and an inclination he traces in the historical development of modern scientific ideas. Contemporary scientists prefer explanations in terms of least parts and Polanyi and Marjorie Grene criticize this as an orientation toward a "one-level

---

[14] Polanyi presumes such a claim is put forth with universal intent, that is, the firm belief that other skilled inquirers too should accept the claim. Polanyi seems to take a position similar to Charles Peirce's claims for that which has reality: real comprehensive entities do not depend merely on what any one knower thinks (which may be a delusional figment) but they are not to be regarded as independent of thought in general; humans are together immersed in thought or inquiry in interpretative communities and future inquiry should illumine the indeterminate future manifestations of real comprehensive entities. Polanyi does suggest, however, that some real comprehensive entities should be regarded as more strongly independent and powerful than other comprehensive entities (see above, Duke IV, 5).

ontology" [68:p4]. Such an orientation is nominalistic and often materialistic. Polanyi suggests in his broader narrative outlining the development of modern ideas that such an orientation ultimately leads to a misrepresentation of science (scientism) and undermines the democratic experiments which the scientific revolution gave rise to and which is the social environment in which Polanyi contended it is most likely that scientific work can flourish.

Here, more specifically, is what Polanyi says about machines as comprehensive entities in PK. He notes that the "logic of contriving" has not been thoroughly explored in philosophy because the reductionist effort to put all knowledge in wholly impersonal terms has blocked the way of inquiry (PK, 328). "Operational principles" can be covered by a patent and can never be known impersonally and such principles are the key to "contrivances" which are objects in which certain operational principles have been embodied (PK, 328). Polanyi suggests that he is loosely thinking of mechanical devices as including machines large and small such as cameras and clocks, telephones and typewriters, boats and locomotives. However, pure scientific inquiry ignores "operational principles", and physics and chemistry cannot even approximately specify any class of contrivances defined by a common operational principle (PK, 329). It is engineers and other technologists, of course, who Polanyi holds are focused on operational principles which must be embodied in materials in order to use such principles to serve certain purposes which engineers and other technologists understand, accept and regard as reasonable. While "rules of rightness" (PK, 329) account for the successful working of machines, the causes of failure must be sought not at the upper level at which certain operational principles tangibly realize a purpose, but at the lower level concerned with the causes of failure of materials which is the basic level at which operate the laws of physics and chemistry. So Polanyi affirms that identifying a machine requires understanding it technically which is a kind of participation in the machine's purpose and an endorsing of the machine's operational principles (PK, 330). He concludes "quite generally that in our knowledge of a comprehensive entity, embodying a rule of rightness, any information supplied by physics and chemistry can play only a subsidiary part" (PK, 331).

In PK, Polanyi applies the same basic reasoning which he applied to machines as comprehensive entities to the case of comprehensive biotic entities. At the beginning of Chapter 11, "The Logic of Achievement," he straightforwardly announces that his argument has several variants and elaborations. But the key notion is that comprehending or understanding a living individual involves subsidiary awareness of parts which cannot be wholly specified in more detailed terms. Understanding is a "molar" or comprehensive achievement and "molar" functions are not specified in "molecular" terms and thus understanding cannot be reduced to its particulars, its molecular elements. Understanding recognizes a higher or more comprehensive form of being which is not determined by its particular elements. This conclusion can be otherwise summarized by saying understanding appreciates the coherence of its subject matter and accepts a value that is not found in constituent particulars themselves (PK 327).

The main difference between the case of comprehensive biotic entities and the case of machines is that, once life begins, living things change in the course of evolutionary history. Evolutionary history Polanyi portrays as the "panorama of emergence" which eventually gives rise to individuals; Polanyi's "spectacle of anthropogenesis" focuses particular attention on human beings who have special talents and tools that can be used to understand life and the cosmos (PK, 389).

In PK, Polanyi emphasizes, in evolutionary history, the importance of the action of principles rather than mutation and random selection which release and sustain the action of principles (PK, 385). As he later succinctly puts matters in his 1964 Duke Lectures, "a principle not noticeably present in the inanimate must come into operation when the inanimate brings forth living things" (Duke IV, 15). With the emergence and operation of this first principle bringing a living system into being comes achievement or failure to achieve (success or failure) which is a matter of ultimacy for a living system.

In PK, Polanyi inextricably weaves together the basic matter of understanding comprehensive entities (mechanical and biotic) and the broader matter of understanding how comprehensive biotic entities change. Living beings are emergents, although Polanyi suggests that he also regards other rich realities (e.g., minds, good problems, scientific discoveries that are comprehensive entities but not comprehensive biotic entities) as emergents. Living beings as emergents develop new levels of control in evolutionary history, and Polanyi portrays new levels of control in terms of the emergence of new principles that become operational. Particularly in PK, Polanyi is especially interested in distinguishing and yet linking mechanical and spontaneous elements in both the emergence of new principles in evolutionary history and morphogenesis. Some Polanyi writing about biotic emergence after PK is clearer than the discussion in PK where emergence in evolutionary history is linked to morphogenesis as well as scientific discovery. These, Polanyi argues, are parallel cases and his ideas about morphogenesis and embryology are particularly speculative ideas based on early scientific work in these areas.[15] In some of

---

[15] Polanyi was interested in the work of Spemann, Driesch, Roux, Waddington and other scientists (PK, 354-359) that opposed simple genetic determinism, but Polanyi died before many of the important developments in what is today called "evo-devo" which have clarified some elements of the intimate connection between development and evolution (see [25]).

his post-PK writing such as his 1968 essay "Life's Irreducible Structure" ([174],included in KB), Polanyi suggests that new principles take root and become operational by degrees in evolutionary history (see KB, 21).

As I have noted above, in the 1966 Wilken interview, Polanyi suggested that by 1962 he believed that he had worked out a new, stronger argument than that found in PK, Part IV. This stronger argument focuses on boundary control, and, in subsequent writing, he often elaborated his account of "dual control" which he applied not only to comprehensive biotic entities but to all comprehensive entities. As he initially notes in "The Structure of Consciousness" ([169], included in KB), he plans in this 1965 essay to show "that a number of different principles can control a comprehensive entity at different levels". and his case can thus be developed "on general lines" (KB, 216). Polanyi argues the conditions under which any principle can be made to operate are wide open and thus a given principle "may be said to form its boundaries, or more precisely its *boundary conditions*" and in "certain cases the boundary conditions of a principle are in fact subject to control by other principles" which are "higher"(KB, 216-217). He gives several examples of control by higher principles including the case of machines,"thus the boundary conditions of the laws of mechanics may be controlled by the operational principle which defines a machine." But in the same way, "the boundary conditions of muscular action may be controlled by a pattern of purposive behaviour" and in the case of playing chess "the conditions left open by the rules of chess are controlled by the stratagems of the players". Thus in these and other cases, comprehensive entities are "subject to dual control" *(*KB, 217).

Polanyi's account of the evolution of comprehensive biotic entities emphasizes the way in which living entities slowly develop more distinct centers and more complicated, integrated or skillfully-used tacit powers; centers deploy tacit powers for more and more complex achievements. In addition to the emergence of principles, Polanyi focuses on tacit integration and its increasing complexity as the key to living agency and the growing scope of living agency.

5.6 Machines and the Human in History

Polanyi has relatively little to say about machines as comprehensive entities immersed in history. He almost certainly assumed machines (the product of human ingenuity) have become more complex and have proliferated in the modern history of technology, but this is not a matter he dwells on. He instead develops an extended account of living agency focusing on evolutionary history. He also outlines, in the larger body of his writing, what might be called an account of responsible human agency, an account that considers human beings as convivial cultural creatures with a broad set of skills (or tacit powers) and the potential to organize life together in ways that provide a humane social order with opportunities for persons to discover callings. The development of machines generally fits into the unfolding account of Polanyi's developmental account of modern society. However, the dispositions of the modern mind Polanyi was sharply critical of and suggested that such dispositions had recently born bitter fruit in the totalitarianism, violence and nihilism of the twentieth century [168]. Although Polanyi called for fundamental reforms in the ways of thinking which grew out of the scientific revolution, he remained both optimistic about society and committed to the cultivation of science and technology to promote human well-being.

To put matters somewhat more directly, machines, in Polanyi's broader account, are one kind of comprehensive entity that human being indwell; we dwell in machines in order to understand, use and improve machines, which ultimately materially change human cultures. Human beings have excelled in using their tacit powers to distribute themselves and construct the niche in which they are embedded.[16] Although he never puts it this way, human beings are social animals who excel in niche-construction. Machines are part of the broader class of human creations which we use to construct our niche.

Polanyi apparently admired the intricacy and elegance of machines and the ingenuity of engineers, but machines are clearly tools. He seems quite deliberately to have avoided suggesting that machines can be regarded as having a

---

[16] Polanyi's writing does not reflect that he was attuned to philosophers commenting specifically on technology and culture like Heidegger, although he does sharply criticize both Marx and the liberal political-economic and philosophical thought to which he takes Marx to be responding. He was an active participant in the vigorous public debate in the thirties and forties about pure and applied science and "planned" science; such discussions were intimately connected to discussions about planned economies and Polanyi's reformed liberal social and economic philosophy was quite critical of much of the enthusiasm for economic planning. In the period after World War I until about 1950, Polanyi frequently contributed to economics discussions and he made an economics education film which he worked hard to promote. Polanyi's ideas about technology and its development are bound up with his ideas about economics and science. Nye provides a solid historical account of the context in which Polanyi's approach to technology as well as his larger philosophical orientation emerge, including the Polanyian roots of some of the more recent discussion in the social studies of science and technology [146, 85-183, 295-307]. To use Feenberg's overly broad typology, Polanyi's comments about machines suggest that he took a more instrumental view of machines and, more generally, technology than a substantive theory of technology [48, 5-8]

center that integrates subsidiaries to realize achievements.[17] Such a conceptual framework he reserves for comprehensive biotic entities which machines resemble in a limited number of ways. Machines tangibly exist (a basic inference) like living beings and are "real" in at least this simplest and least significant sense. To understand a machine draws upon what I above have called the bodily dimension of a tacit knower. To know a machine requires indwelling. But machines as real things apparently do not have a rich polyvalent dimension as do real things such as other human persons or complex problems and theories. Like comprehensive biotic entities, machines operate as "dual control" systems.[18] That is, a machine has a lower level of control (most frequently characterized by Polanyi in terms of its conformity to the laws of

---

[17] Héder and Paksi argue [79, 9] that the development of autonomous robots calls for amending Polanyi's conceptual framework: autonomous robots have "regulative functions" which suggest such robots do have a "centre" which effectively controls the robot. While I understand some of the problems contemporary autonomous robots raise, it nevertheless seems clear that Polanyi scrupulously avoided applying the terminology used to describe living beings (i.e., center, achievement, and knowledge in particular) to machines, even if what is signified by such terms when applied to machines is rather different than when such terms are applied to living systems (as Héder and Paksi suggest). In his more general discussion of automation in PK (PK, 261-262), Polanyi perhaps did anticipate the development of more complex machines, but he does not hint that the conceptual framework used to describe comprehensive biotic entities can be adapted for such innovations in engineering. He noted, in a PK discussion, that he was shifting his discussion to the "wider problem raised by gunsight predictors, automatic pilots, etc." or, more broadly, to "machines whose performances range far beyond logical inferences" (PK, 261).

[18] Machines as dual control systems are telic devices. If their purposes change (i.e., if new higher operational principles come to control boundaries left open, it appears that Polanyi thinks this is the doing of human agents, but perhaps more recent digital devices challenge this assumption. Comprehensive biotic entities are, unlike machines, embedded autonomous systems in which dual control seems to evolve since such systems are embedded in a dynamic niche. That is, new levels of control "emerge" or "evolve." Héder and Paksi in their reflection on autonomous robots [79, 8-14] seem to think of "emergence" not so much in terms of the arrival of new levels of control, but primarily in terms of the way in which a higher level of operational principles is instantiated in the margin left undetermined by lower levels in a machine. Thus a machine is an emergent entity, a peculiar kind of complexity in the natural landscape. The matter of whether such an entity changes, Héder and Paksi perhaps think is not relevant to whether or not is it an "emergent" entity. My discussion of Polanyi's account of comprehensive entities emphasizes that Polanyi was interested not only in boundary control but the way in which new principles come into play. At least this is the case with comprehensive biotic entities if not other kinds of comprehensive entities which are resonantly real. Machines that "learn" perhaps also evolve I am suggesting.

physics and chemistry) and, in the boundaries or margins left open, a higher engineering operational principle is established and this makes the machine a purposeful device producing some desirable commodity. Polanyi does imply that some complex machines have several dual controlled layers and such a machine is thus a complex hierarchy just as more sophisticated comprehensive biotic entities. The higher level of control always operates in margins left open by the next lower level and functions to add definition or a refined purpose to a device. But machines, according to Polanyi, are a fixed set of relationships that produce successful output in terms of rules of rightness.

5.7 Polanyi on Digital Computers

When he was preparing his Gifford Lectures (delivered in 1951 and 1952), Polanyi was also a participant in a 1949 academic conference focusing on cybernetics and particularly on "the question of whether machines can be said to think" [162:p312]. This at least was the question that interested Polanyi and it was a question to which he answered a resounding "no." The discussions of this conference spilled over into 1951 and 1952 publications in the *British Journal of the Philosophy of Science* (vol. 2) and articles in other journals. Under the title "The Hypothesis of Cybernetics," Polanyi published a concise three-page discussion comment (partially incorporated in PK, 261-263) which makes a case that it is a "logical fallacy" to claim "the operations of a formalized deductive system might conceivably be considered equivalent to the operations of the mind" [162:p312]. Essentially, Polanyi argues that formalized deductive systems rely on a human user's reliance on "unformalised" [162:p312] skillful elements and assumptions (he might later have called these tacit elements): " a formal system of symbols and operations functions in a deductive system only by virtue of unformalised supplements" and thus it is the case that " we must know the meaning of undefined terms, understand what is stated in our axioms and believe it to be true, and acknowledge an implication in the handling of symbols by formal proof" [162:p313]. Polanyi calls these unformalized but important elements "the 'semantic operations' of the formalized system" [162:p312]. He points out that formalization can be extended and it may be a worthy goal to reduce informal functions but they cannot be eliminated and it is folly to aim to do so. Semantic operations are functions of a skillful human mind that understands and operates a formal system: "A formalized deductive system is an instrument which requires for its completion a mind using the instrument in a manner not fully determined by the instrument; while the mind of the person using the instrument requires no such logical completion" [162:p313-314].

What Polanyi says in "The Hypothesis of Cybernetics" meshes seamlessly with the constructive philosophical account, his "fiduciary program," set forth in his 1951 and 1952 Gifford Lectures and later in *Personal Knowledge*.[19] Polanyi's constructive "fiduciary" philosophy is woven with (in both his Gifford Lectures and *Personal Knowledge*) his effort to set forth shortcomings of other contemporary philosophical perspectives oriented exclusively to the explicit. I can note here only a few of Polanyi's important constructive philosophical claims. The fourth lecture of Series I is titled "The Fiduciary Mode" and it aims to "recast declaratory statements into a form which makes it apparent that they are personal allegations (Fiduciary Mode)." This account of declaratory statements "brings them into line with other personal actions and should eventually lead to a justification of declaratory statements within a general framework of personal commitment" (Syllabus for Series I). Particularly "The Hypothesis of Cybernetics" fits with the Series II sixth lecture titled "Skills and Connoisseurship" a version of which was published soon after its November 1952 delivery in Aberdeen in a proceedings volume for a methodological studies conference (sponsored by an Italian center for methodological studies).[20] Polanyi identifies his purpose as to extend the "survey of our personal knowledge further, beyond the facts controlled by any definite formalism into the domain of skills and connoisseurships" [163:p381]. He shows the pervasiveness of connoisseurships and human skills which are "inarticulate performances" in which human commitment "is inherent in the structure of these performances" and thus this "necessarily makes us both participate in their achievement and acknowledge their results" [163:p381]. Polanyi's discussion sets forth important distinctions between the "different categories of personal knowledge" ([163:p389] e.g., motoric skills, pattern recognition, and connoisseurship). He acknowledges the movement in modernity to replace connoisseurship operating in science and technology when possible with "measured grading" [163:p391]; this produces more consistent results in different hands in different places. He notes that "the greater diffusibility of articulate as compared with unspecifiable knowledge is striking" [163:p387].

---

[19] See my extended discussion of "The Fiduciary Program" in "An Introduction to Michael Polanyi's Gifford Lectures" (3-6) available online (cited in endnote 2 above) with the Gifford Lectures. Also available in the same location is the "Syllabus for Series I" (also cited in endnote 2 above); quotations from the "Syllabus for Series I" are noted simply in parenthesis.
[20] Polanyi apparently participated in this conference held December 17-20, [163]. I cite here this publication rather than the heavily redacted Gifford Lecture version. This presentation is an important basis for the PK "Skills" chapter (PK, 49-64); much of it is incorporated (PK, xvi identifies PK, 49-57) but the Polanyi,1952b essay and the Gifford Lecture include some interesting things not developed in PK, 49-64.

But Polanyi also suggests that "undefinable knowledge" cannot be eliminated in science and technology and tradition and apprenticeships remain central to science and technology.

In Chapter 8 of PK, "The Logic of Affirmation," Polanyi somewhat expanded the views articulated in his original Series II sixth lecture and "The Hypothesis of Cybernetics" in his discussion of inference, automation, neurology and psychology (PK, 257-263). He adds a discussion of Gödel's work as providing very important theorems which show the limits of formalization in logical thought (PK, 259). Polanyi contends Gödel made clear that uncertainty can be eliminated in any particular deductive system when there is a shift to a wider system of axioms and this may allow proving the consistency of the original system. However, such proof will remain uncertain because the consistency of the broader system of axioms will be uncertain (PK, 259). Polanyi's general claim in PK is very similar to that made in earlier writing: "a formal system of symbols and operations can be said to function as a deductive system only by virtue of unformalized supplements, to which the operator of the system accedes" and he calls these necessary unformalized elements "the *semantic functions* of the formal system" (PK, 258). He contends that to hold a logical inference machine itself draws inferences is logically absurd. Human beings accredit such machines and accept as their own the inferences such machines draw in operations. Formalization reduces tacit coefficients to more limited and obvious informal operations and this is a legitimate purpose of formalization. But formalization never totally eliminates "our personal participation," and it is, in fact, preposterous to aim at total elimination (PK, 259).

In his more general discussion of automation in PK, Polanyi suggested he was shifting to the broader problems of automation moving beyond logical inference machines. He argues the "necessary relatedness of machines to persons does essentially restrict the independence of a machine and reduce the status of automata in general below that of thinking persons" (PK, 261-262). Effectively this means (as his earlier writing affirmed) there is a fundamental difference between a human being and a machine: "A man's mind can carry out feats of intelligence *by aid of* a machine and also *without* such , while a machine can function only as the extension of a person's body under the control of his mind" (PK, 262). In Polanyi's complementary discussion of neurology and psychology in PK (262-263), he argues that a human being with a mind can know things either focally or subsidiarily, but a machine can not do this. A mind is "not the aggregate of its focally known manifestations, but is that on which we focus our attention while being subsidiarily aware of its manifestations" (PK, 263). Thus minds but not machines can be said "to think, feel, imagine, desire, mean, believe or judge something" (PK, 263). While machines may simulate these propensities and may even deceive human beings, deception does not make machines equivalent to minds; Polanyi thus rejected the Turing test (PK, 263, n. 1).

5.8 Machines that "Learn": Moving Beyond Polanyi

In the time after Polanyi was writing, digital devices have proliferated and are much more sophisticated today.[21] Polanyi's "post-critical" era, given the development of digital tools, is a time of emerging digital culture. I have elsewhere speculated that the late twentieth century and the early decades of the twenty-first century can fruitfully be compared to the early transitional phases of manuscript culture and book culture (i.e., the age of the incunabula). Today is a time in which many human mental habits are being reformed through our use of new digital tools to extend ourselves into the world in order to manipulate it and understand it [134, 135].The electronic networked world has brought an astronomical proliferation of digital artifacts many of which are readily accessible. Do Polanyi's now fifty-year-old conclusions about computing devices as the latest version of the machine today seem on the mark? This is a broad question worth considering in today's emerging digital culture.

In the middle of the last century, Polanyi, understandably, did not anticipate in any detail the ways in which the digital computer appears now to be an epoch-making device [13]. Nevertheless, some of his basic claims seem sound. Computers remain machines whose successful use generally depends on what Polanyi early called "unformalised supplements" [162:p313] supplied by human users. That is, there are inevitably certain external configurations and affirmations Polanyi called "semantic functions" (PK, 258) connected with the use of a computer to address what a person initially discerns as a problem worth scrutiny and later entertains as a plausible result.[22] But ques-

---

[21] For non-experts like the present writer, the 41 episodes of Crash Course Computer Science (particularly some of the later episodes) produced by PBS Digital Studio available on YouTube [151] provide helpful background.

[22] In an odd way, Polanyi mid-century comments about unspecifiable skills and connoisseurship also seem prescient. Although he noted skills and connoisseurship are pervasive, cannot be fully eliminated, and always already have embedded in them human commitment, he also recognized the expansion of "measured grading" [163, 1952b], which produces articulate knowledge that promotes science and technology. Polanyi's 1952 essay provides a rich discussion of the extraordinary skills and connoisseurship of human cotton graders (who he clearly respected); very likely his discussion was rooted in firsthand experience with graders when he was a chemist working on cotton at the Kaiser Wilhelm Institutes. However, for a glimpse at contemporary multi-faceted cotton grading, look at the 24-page online booklet "The Classification of Cotton," produced by Cotton Incorporated, an industry group working with the approval of and using the standards set up by the US

tions about whether computers can be designed to function with a more deeply embedded internal semantic component are important today, and the issues seem to move beyond the conceptual framework Polanyi set forth for thinking about computers as machines.

I agree with Jean Bocharova's claim that Polanyi's mid-century interest was intensely focused on logic, formalization and the limits of formalization [9:p22]. The several quotations from his writing in the last section clearly show this. Bocharova convincingly argues that Polanyi's criticism of neural models based on early brain-as-a-computer ideas (i.e., focusing on "symbolic processing, with preprogrammed and sequential steps, local storage of memory and discrete packets of information" [9:p21]) don't seem to apply to more recent connectionist brain models and neurobiology that focuses on parallel distributed processing and patterns [9:p21-22]. Polanyi may have been pursuing an early path moving generally in this connectionist direction, as his interest in embryology, morphology and figures like Waddington suggests, but he does not move far down this path which in his era was in fact not yet much of a path. Polanyi seems to have thought about the operation of digital computers and computer neural models exclusively in terms of a set of predetermined rules functioning automatically in terms of a fixed set of relations. Polanyi's mode of reflection seems to be a strictly contrastive mode: that is, he outlines an account of comprehensive biotic entities suggesting how new operational principles emerge in evolutionary history[23] and this account is a polar opposite account to that of machines (including computing devices) as comprehensive entities understood as dual control systems in which there are only fixed relations. Although Polanyi's account of the computer and using a computer seem in some ways correct, what he does not seem to have anticipated is the development of complex algorithms which can "learn."

Department of Agriculture [32]. This booklet reports that only the very difficult classifications for extraneous matter entwined in cotton strands and special conditions still rely on human senses and are performed manually; current research continues in order to provide instruments to measure these factors which will complete the transition to an all instrument classification system. Human beings are, of course, still involved at a certain level in the objectified, instrument-implemented, precise industrial process of grading cotton and they have confidence in the system created. Whether the use of and spread of such relatively autonomous systems inevitably promotes notions about the ideal of explicit knowledge as the only kind of human knowledge seems to me an interesting question in contemporary culture.

[23] A major, persisting philosophical interest of Polanyi was countering what he took to be the prevailing perspective in philosophy of biology based largely on the modern synthesis. See [138] for a discussion.

In contemporary economically developed cultures, digital devices using algorithms that "learn" are becoming common. Every media platform today regularly features discussions of "artificial intelligence" and the anticipated ways more widespread uses of "intelligent" devices are beginning to affect—and will more decisively affect—life and culture.[24] "Artificial intelligence" is, of course, an ambiguous notion, but at least some of this domain today is concerned with potential uses of algorithms that "learn," which sometimes are identified as deep neural networks. North Americans are beginning to become accustomed to finding that sophisticated algorithms can and are being used to probe matters that are difficult and delicate for human beings to probe. At least some contemporary media discussions of the use of sophisticated algorithms try both to explain and to ask searching questions about these devices and their power to shape lives and communities. A January, 2018 *New York Times* story carefully analyzes the effective use of a predictive analytic algorithm by a Pittsburg children's welfare office to refine the judgements of call screeners who must decide if case workers should immediately visit stressed families (who already are involved with the legal system) in which there seems great potential for child neglect or abuse [91]. There are, of course, all sorts of privacy and other political liberty questions embedded in the use of such an algorithm, but the discussion of the development and use of this non-proprietary algorithm has been relatively transparent. It is clear that the use of the algorithm can prompt helpful human interventions in cases in which the judgement of a skilled human screener does not pick up enough cues to justify an intervention that will protect vulnerable children. Another recent *New York Times* story written by an oncologist describes a sophisticated algorithm that has consumed mountains of digital medical data and can now predict more accurately than most physicians when a terminally ill patient is likely to die [133]. This is important information that can have a direct impact on the quality of palliative care. Voice recognition software is increasingly common in North American consumer products. Smartphones like the I-Phone with "Siri" coupled with GPS provide directions and virtual personal assistants, such as Amazon's inexpensive "Alexa," can be instructed to turn on the lights or radio or provide a reminder message (if the BOT is properly linked to Wi-Fi) with a voice command.

---

[24] The brief discussion in the remainder of this paragraph is intended only to suggest the scope of contemporary "AI" discussions and experience. Clearly, there are many media reports unlike the *New York Times* stories mentioned here that are quite foreboding. See, for example, Bill Godwin's ComputerWeekly.com online story suggesting the multiplication of "AI weeds" (i.e., low level AI software) operating on the internet soon could choke available bandwidth [63].

Complex, powerful algorithms that can "learn" are algorithms that have the "capacity of improvising and improving;" they are designed and programmed to "optimise operations over certain objectives by learning on the job" [226:p2].[25] Many such algorithms are deep neural networks with many hidden layers which are organized to take full advantage of the speed, vast storage, and abundant data available (to be analyzed) in contemporary computing environments (i.e., in digital culture). Deep neural networks work off probability and correlation much more than early approaches [105:p48]. A machine learning algorithm can "tweak itself" by employing a great variety of new techniques: "Machine learning isn't just one technique. It encompasses entire families of them, from 'boosted decision trees,' which allow an algorithm to change the weighting it gives to each data point, to 'random forests,' which average together many thousands of randomly generated decision trees" [105:p49]. Deep neural networks thus employ an approach different than that used for early expert systems which focused on trying to provide an exhaustive set of rules which could be recombined. Deep neural networks employ techniques "for letting machines find their own patterns in the data" [105:p50]. Because deep neural networks are relatively opaque—human beings cannot easily see what such networks are teaching themselves—a new area of research "called explainable A.I. or X.A.I." has recently emerged with

---

[25] Yajnik suggests, invoking Polanyi, that the "capacity for improvising and improving" could be regarded as a machine acquiring "Dynamic Tacit knowledge" and this "could be considered an essential criterion for an AI agent." Following [145], Yajnik misconstrues Polanyi's "explicit" and "tacit" as exclusive categories of knowledge (articulate and inarticulate). Thus he claims traditional machines are unconscious and can have only tacit knowledge. But contemporary computers that run algorithms with deep learning capacity produce improvisation, which can be regarded as having dynamic tacit knowledge. Although Yajnik's Polanyian conceptual framework is scrambled, his general point is an interesting one. For Polanyi, tacit knowing is a process in living beings in which that which can function tacitly grows and changes—the tacit dimension is thus dynamic. Thus human improvisation and learning are fundamentally linked to the human use of a growing body of skills and suppositions functioning tacitly or subsidiarily. Yajnik seems in some ways on the right track in characterizing deep learning algorithms as manifesting something like the machine equivalent of tacit knowledge. See my discussion below. I am indebted to recent e-mail exchanges with Eduardo Beira and Jean Bocharova for insights about how deep neural networks might be something like a machine equivalent of what Polanyi calls in human beings "tacit knowledge." I am also indebted to Mihály Héder for interesting comments on a first draft of this essay. He provided a copy of [79] which argues autonomous robots have a kind of tacit knowledge.

the goal of making "machines able to account for the things they learn" in ways that human beings can understand [105:p48].

Some contemporary discussion about machine learning algorithms seems to challenge Polanyi's ideas about dual control in machines and in particular, the way in which Polanyi portrays dual controlled machines as a sharp contrast to the evolving dual control in comprehensive biotic entities. Living beings change in evolutionary history as selection and mutation release the action of new principles which become sustained operational habits. Such new higher principles operate in living creatures (giving further shape or definition) by controlling boundary conditions of the next lower level. But Polanyi does not seem to have envisioned that machines could evolve in a way comparable to the way comprehensive biotic entities evolve. However, if a deep learning algorithm (which human beings, of course, originally design) can reframe or enhance objectives by finding its own patterns in data, this seems at least akin to Polanyi's claims for emergence in comprehensive biotic entities (if not also other richly real comprehensive entities such as good problems with indeterminate future manifestations). A new level of control apparently can come into play in the functioning of a deep neural network. In Polanyi's conceptual framework, such a new level might be regarded as an emergent principle that comes to control boundary conditions of a lower level of control. This new level of control perhaps arises from machine assessments of probability and correlation, but it nevertheless seems to be an emergent.

Does the operation of deep learning algorithms in contemporary computing environments mean that machines now have something like what Polanyi regarded as the "tacit knowledge" (or, better stated, tacit powers or tacit skills) in human beings and other comprehensive biotic entities? This question seems akin to matters concerned with the emergence of new levels of control in deep learning algorithms. Polanyi provided an integrational model of human knowing, one that fundamentally challenged the dominant emphasis upon knowledge as explicit in the history of Western philosophy (and particularly in modern science and philosophy of science); Polanyi shifted the philosophical discussion to emphasize how anything explicitly known relies on that which is tacit or subsidiary for a person. It is the from-to personal dynamic of knowing that Polanyi's thought makes primary. The development of deep learning algorithms in no way undermines Polanyi's account of personal knowledge, but it does suggest that the results of some contemporary machine processes may be more akin to human knowing than Polanyi anticipated.

Polanyi argues that animals other than human beings have tacit powers, but they lack complex articulation skills and complex language tools that human beings have developed to become biocultural creatures. Thus, while certainly some other living creatures can direct attention and respond by integrating tacitly known particulars, they do not have a complex articulate culture. Human powers of articulation and the technology of writing make possible a complex cultural community. The development and proliferation of digital computers and the proliferation of digital artifacts—the growth of digital culture—is a recent human achievement reflecting new developments in the technology of writing. The arrival of machines that "learn" should be studied and evaluated in the context of this new step in the broader technology of writing rather than simply in the largely engineering and evolutionary biology context in which Polanyi seems to have framed the issues in the last century.[26]

---

[26] Albert Borgmann's work as a philosopher of technology poses a fundamental question about digital culture: are digital tools simply a new technology which should be understood in terms of further encroachment of the dominant "device paradigm" [16:p76-78] that commodifies more and more focal things and practices which in earlier human culture gave human life depth and meaning? Borgmann is wary of many digital tools and suspects that much of the new digital technology is a slippery slope into hyperreality [17:p78-126]. He calls for recovering the balance between the natural and cultural ecologies of signs and the increasingly dominant ecology of digital signs emerging in digital culture [18:p57]. Borgmann's cautionary note deserves serious attention, although I believe the ways in which digital technology has transformed human life are predominantly positive or at least have enormous positive potential. Computing understood generically is a tool for the human construction and configuring of digital artifacts; some of these artifacts are used to construct humane cultures and the material basis to sustain human life. Computing so understood is a new chapter in writing technology. Machines that "learn" seem to be a new page in this new chapter. Polanyi's philosophical framework for envisioning machines is helpful for understanding basic elements of the symbiotic relation of persons and machines. But, as I have suggested, it seems that today a richer account of machines using evolutionary algorithms in digital culture is needed.

Chapter 6

Michael Polanyi and the Epistemology of Engineering

Mihály Héder

Budapest University of Technology and Economics

Summary

In his main monograph, Michael Polanyi promotes a new philosophy, the "fiduciary program," which is meant to tackle problems facing humanity. At its core, there is a new epistemology called Personal Knowledge, which is also the title of the book. This includes a comprehensive description of the epistemology of engineering as a distinct mode of knowing with its own characteristics, along with Polanyi's other two categories, "natural" and "exact" sciences.

In this article, Polanyi's engineering epistemology is reconstructed and evaluated. Polanyi states that all knowledge is either tacit or rooted in the tacit, and also explains how it originated from inarticulate animal knowledge. The knowledge of engineers is rooted in evolution in what Polanyi calls Type A learning, which involves a heuristic act of contrivance. For animals, this is essential for discovering means-ends-relationships.

For human engineers, the situation is not at all different. They harbor a particular kind of intellectual passion, the heuristic passion for discovering novel and economic ways of achieving goals.

What they discover are certain kinds of rules of rightness: operational principles of machines. This concept is part of Polanyi's hierarchical ontology. According to Polanyi, our material world has multiple levels of existence. Some things—living organizations and machines— are more real than everything else, because they are not merely material: they are emergent. In Polanyi's view, there is nothing extraordinary about these entities, as they are part of nature. As such, they should be accounted for by science just like any other phenomena. And, in fact, science does this, but it does not reflect this fact because it tends to employ a faulty methodology.

Emergent entities come into existence—or emerge—from matter. This is possible because the laws of matter leave room for higher level laws—rules of rightness—to operate. In the context of machines, these higher-level laws are called operational principles. The correctly implemented machine can operate flawlessly as long as the material conditions do not deteriorate outside limits.

The knowledge of the engineer is about these rules of rightness. From this, it follows that discovery in engineering means finding new operational principles. But the rules of rightness cannot account for faulty behavior. Failures always have material causes; therefore, the engineering profession entails a good grasp of material sciences. I will argue that this approach can be the conceptual basis for basic engineering research that is in contrast with applied science, the category engineering usually falls into.[1]

6.1 Introduction

This article extracts the aspects relevant for engineering epistemology from Michael Polanyi's main philosophical work. This monograph [175], titled *Personal Knowledge: Towards a Post-Critical Philosophy* (PK from this point) offers a completely novel, all-encompassing epistemology and also bold ontological statements. In this article, I don't rely much on any other Polanyi sources, except *Life's Irreducible Structure* [174] and *The Structure of Consciousness* [166]. Also, I refer to the work of Phil Mullins about *Michael Polanyi on Machines as Comprehensive Entities* [139] in the same volume this article appears an on Esther Meek's *Contact With Reality* [120]. The main reason for this is that there appears to be no major shifts in his thinking about the issues relevant to us - his subsequent works all tend to the same direction as set out in PK only in more detail and an altered terminology.

Polanyi aims to update the core of what we think about the nature and status of all knowledge in general. As the nature of knowing is at the foundations of all domains of knowledge, every profession is affected by this update. Polanyi is conscious about this situation, and explicitly mentions biology and other natural sciences, social science, history, mathematics, art and engineering, too.

The phrase "post-critical" in the subtitle summarizes the main statement very well. That is: while the critical, objectivist approach - Polanyi uses these terms broadly to portray all approaches that attempt to remove the *personal coefficient* from knowing - in epistemology has been a tremendously useful for humanity, it

---

[1] This article was supported by the János Bolyai Research Scholarship of the Hungarian Academy of Sciences and the ÚNKP-18-4 New National excellence Program of the Ministry of Human Capacities.

only succeeded because it has never been exercised in a perfectly systematic manner, leaving room for uncritical elements in the production of knowledge.

Since these uncritical elements are there by necessity, the efforts to remove them are bound to fail and sometimes produce negative side effects. These include making scientists mislead themselves and everybody else about the origin and status of their knowledge through moves that Polanyi calls *deceptive substitutions*; also in a broader social setting, the same systematic, maximally critical attitude inhibits the reflection on human passions that, of course, remain just as vigorous regardless of our awareness of them, leading to *moral inversion*. This in turn, in Polanyi's evaluation, is a contributing factor to the horrors of historical catastrophes, like those in the twentieth century in the two world wars and communism. To heal these very destructive forces and events, Polányi offers the *fiduciary program*.

6.2 Ontology in Personal Knowledge

Polányi's conceptual system in PK, as he himself admits it, is circular on the explicit level. In order to justify this situation, he explains that on a conceptual level, only circular systems of beliefs are possible - no one has any other kind of conceptual system.

In this case, Polányi suggests, those systems that reflect on their own circularity are more valuable for their honesty than those that pretend to have independent foundations but in reality are just as circular.

In Polanyi's account, animals have evolved to have an usually reliable grasp of reality as the opposite was not good for survival. Humanity, at the most advanced end of the spectrum of animals, therefore is usually right to rely on its skills in knowing reality [120].

It is evident that other animals don't use language and therefore their knowledge can be nothing else but tacit [81]. Human knowledge is also rooted in the tacit and can only ever be partially explicit. The consequence of these statements is that it is possible for humans to learn the truth about reality, but what they learn is always reliant on tacit knowledge and thus cannot pass wholly explicit tests or verification, and therefore relying on such tests as anything more than heuristic tools in knowledge production is an error in methodology. These tests of objectivity and experimental verification can never become such final arbiters of knowledge as they are sometimes expected to be.

Now, Polanyi's ontology is proposed in this modality. The following set of ontological statements is based on several scientists' work as well as Polanyi's own understanding of the world - but the fact that this is a good description of the world is on an explicit level only supported by the fact that this is how humans tend to understand it.

In nature, there are *ordering principles* in effect. These govern all non-random phenomena, which sometimes are labelled as *systems* by Polanyi. *"When I say that an event is governed by chance, I deny that it is governed by order"* (PK, p34).

An example of a natural phenomenon governed by ordering principles is the *"movement of planets around the sun* (PK p39)" Ordering principles have a subset called operational principles. These describe the *"correct functioning"* (PKp346) of entities that have a *"teleological character"* (PKp381).

The main statement about these entities is that they are of a class of things defined by a common operational principle and unspecifiable by the laws of physics and chemistry. (PKp346)

These entities include machines and living beings that are "classed with machines" [174]. Therefore these entities are the subject of engineering and biology, respectively. These disciplines investigate the operational principles in order to explain successful functioning and fall back to physics and chemistry to explain failures. He says the operational principles of machines are, therefore *"rules of rightness"*. (PKp346)

Where entities governed by plain ordering principles end and where entities governed by operational principles begin (see in the figure below) is never fully specified by Polanyi. But it is possible to find an example of the simplest machines, which is the gas flame:

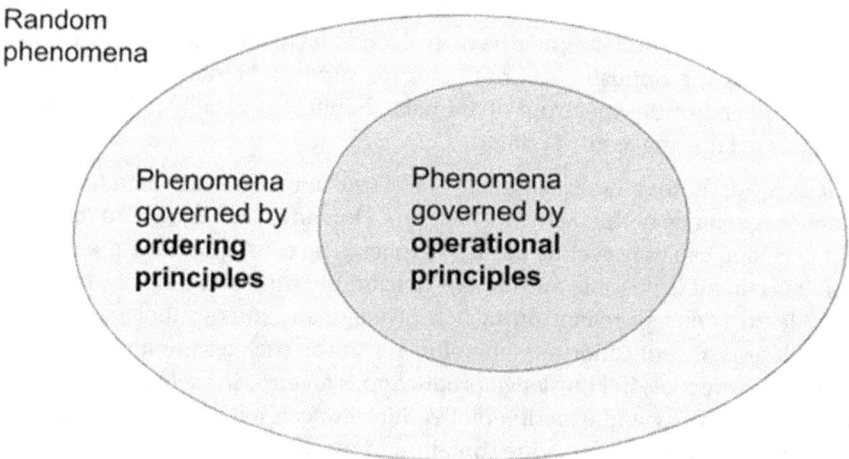

"() its identity is not defined by its physical or chemical topography, but by the operational principles which sustain it." (PKp406)

Other examples offered are *cybernetics, typewriters, clocks, boats, telephones, locomotives, cameras* (PKp345)

6.3 Dual Control

These entities emerge from the physico-chemical level of existence to a higher level (see the explanation below at the "intensity of coherent existence"). The resulting situation is what Polanyi calls *dual control* in his 1965 essay Structure of Consciousness [169]. In order for the system to function properly, by its operational principles, the physical-chemical environment, as well as the parts of the system, needs to be within certain physico-chemical limits. These conditions enable the governance of the operational principles and therefore the explanation of the success of the entity requires these principles. The situation is explained in detail by [139].

However, failure is to be explained by physics and chemistry, and as a deviation from the necessary conditions or obstacles that prevent the successful work of operational principles.

Therefore, there are two different kinds of conditions operating on different levels. Both sets are necessary for the machine-like entity's proper functioning. Hence, the situation is controlled by both, as the term *dual control* suggests.

6.4 Operational Principles and Life

In case of living beings, the operational principles in question are researched by biology, but the dual control situation is the same: *"[a] machine-like function is characterized by its operational principle, (...). Therefore, as an organism sustains itself by functioning as a machine, it is the embodiment of an ordering principle that cannot be defined in terms of physics and chemistry."* (PKp426)

Moreover, there is an explicit link between technology and life, as *"every manifestation of life is a technical achievement, and is therefore - like the practice of technology - an applied knowledge of nature."* (PKp426)

The examples for operational principles of life are equilibration (PKp359) during embryonic development, organ development, metabolism but also the more advanced forms of self-regulation like identifying food or prey and thriving to reproduce.

6.5 From Ontology to Epistemology

As we progress from randomness through ordering principles to operational principles, we see higher and higher *"intensity of coherent existence"* (PKp39).

Living things, especially animals themselves are examples of more coherently existing entities and, at the same time, their survival usually depends on recognizing other such entities. Moreover, in order to survive, they need to learn about how such entities behave, either as prey, dangerous predators, or tools. For animals, this knowledge is entirely tacit. Humans are able to express and transmit their knowledge, but only partially. Yet, as Polanyi explains, this ability gave the gift of cultural inheritance.

Part of this inheritance is the sciences. The structure of knowledge of sciences reflects their subject [139]. Therefore engineering and biology contain teleological elements and the study of operational principles. Attempts to transform these disciplines (Polanyi discusses biology, but we can infer to engineering science as well), to be more like physics and chemistry - especially by removing the teleological element - have been damaging and if done systematically it results in a loss of grip on reality.

And just as the teleological element cannot be sensibly removed from these disciplines, the so-called *intellectual passions* should be preserved too. These again are rooted in animal passions like the drive by hunger, self-preservation and reproduction. As with knowledge, Polanyi sees continuity between animals and humans and human scientists in this respect, too. The scientists possess the *selective passion*, which helps to tell apart the interesting phenomena, theories and directions from the non-interesting ones and is a remote descendant of the selective mechanisms of animals, e.g., during hunting or searching for food. There is a kind of passion that facilitates problem-solving in both engineering and science and can be traced back to the heuristic capabilities that can be shown in animal experiments. These experiments reveal what Polanyi calls Type A learning, which involves a *heuristic act of contrivance*. For animals, this is essential for discovering means-ends-relationships.

For human engineers, the situation is not at all different. They harbor a particular kind of intellectual passion, the *heuristic passion* for discovering novel and economic ways for achieving goals.

Finally, there is the *persuasive passion* that drives the scientist to try and share his or her knowledge and convince others about the discovered truth, which is again traced back to the feeling of the comfort of conviviality already present in the animal kingdom.

6.6 Engineering epistemology

Based on the previous discussion, engineering is a form of *contrivance*. The subject of this contrivance is finding *operational principles* and *explaining failures*, often with physics and chemistry. Its subjects are *dual-controlled machines*. Engineering can be mostly associated with the *heuristic passion* but also draws on all intellectual passions.

Naturally, like all domains of knowledge, engineering heavily on *tacit knowledge*. Because of the nature of operational principles, it is necessarily teleological. This *teleological* nature is also the reason why it is often identified as *normative*: if the goal is to create a machine, the operational principles become prescriptions for what to do, for how to achieve the proper functioning.

Also, we can establish that engineering is not just Applied Science (where "science" means physics, chemistry - as is often implied in English but less so in other languages). True, natural science is a necessary part of engineering used in explaining failures and investigating the physico-chemical preconditions of operational principles. But a major part of engineering is about these principles themselves about which physics and chemistry cannot say anything. This enables the viability of *basic engineering research*, which concerns operational principles.

6.7 Summary

Polanyi does not aim to say novel things about the philosophy of engineering in particular. He intends to reform all domains of knowledge, including engineering about which he consciously formulates some key statements. Both epistemic and ontological elements are provided for understanding the field.

The fact that there are different intensities of existence in Polanyi's account means that this is a multi-layered ontology, but one which is emergent on matter. This provides us with the concept of the dual-controlled emergent machine that is both based on matter and governed by operational principles. This is the subject of engineering and its characteristics should be reflected in the nature of engineering knowledge - containing teleological knowledge and material laws.

Just like any field of human knowledge, engineering relies on intellectual passions, mostly the heuristic passion which drives problem-solving, a focal activity of engineering.

Part III - Aesthetic Approaches

Chapter 7

Essays on Aesthetic Approaches

Anna Caterina Dalmasso, Jacopo Bodini, Mihály Héder

Screens have become the interfaces through which we encounter the world and others. As such, they work more and more as bodily prostheses enhancing and extending human perception, knowledge and action. Indeed, the coupling of body and screens has never been so evident as in the last decades, by virtue of the diffusion of wearable devices and augmented reality technologies.

As it has been pointed out by several studies, such a massive exteriorisation of human capacities into technologies could also entail the risk of a dematerialization of the bodily experience and even engender a progressive insensibilisation of our perceptive, cognitive and relational functions.

This is why an interrogation about technology and especially about embodied technics becomes urgent to account for the anthropological transformations that are afoot in contemporary technoculture. Should we infer then that the screen would lead to an elision of the living body presence as we know it? Are our technologized bodies becoming themselves prosthesis of media? Or, are we simply facing a further stage of the exteriorization of technics, in which Leroi-Gourhan saw the very germ of human evolution?

Despite the digital revolution having originated unprecedented configurations, we still tend to describe them by means of categories of the past – such as subject/object, activity/passivity, nature/culture – which leads to opposing the screen and the body as separate and antithetic entities. To encompass this dualism, we need to elaborate a new theoretical paradigm enabling us to understand our bodily experience in its essential links – rather than in its supposed opposition – to our technoculture.

Thus, the contributions of this section address technology in its connection with our embodied experience, as their relationship inflects and catalyses changes in our sensorium and desire, reconfiguring images of our body and transforming identities.

In his chapter, Jacopo Bodini explores the nature of the screen. He does this in a very speculative and technologically highly evolved sense which considers even the yet unrealized possibilities of virtual reality and their significance for our lives. He first reviews his approach according to which screens might become prostheses of our bodies:

> "With Bernard Stiegler's philosophy of technics, we can understand prosthesis not as an object or a tool added – in a secondary moment – to an organic and systematic body, that comes first; but rather as something that co-originates itself with the human being".

Then, he turns everything on its head and claims that the screen itself might be a body - albeit without organs and therefore relying on our body parts as prostheses.

In her paper, Anna Caterina Dalmasso suggests, drawing on Simondon and Merleau-Ponty, that in order to engage with the world humans rely on their aesthetic abilities, which are rooted in the very nature of their bodies. This, in turn, implies that technological thinking, as an attitude has a deeply aesthetic dimension.

> "Therefore, if we read Simondon in the prism of Merleau-Ponty's account of technics, we can even push further his conception of techno-aesthetics by extending it to the very structure of the human body, of technics in the flesh."

Having made this connection, she explores the consequences: namely that because the relationship between the aesthetic attitude and technology is bi-directional, technicity might very well affect how humans perceive themselves, their surroundings and how they live within their interpersonal relationships.

Chapter 8

The Screen: a Body Without Organs

Jacopo G. Bodini

Univeristé Jean Moulin Lyon 3

Summary

In an episode of the Netflix series Black Mirror, a device applied to the temple of the brain allows old people to temporary explore a parallel dimension as tourists by using their old, sick bodies as screens that project them into young, functioning bodies. The place where they go, San Junipero, is a virtual world: a massive database in the cloud to which people, instead of dying, can upload their consciousness. The difference between the tourists and the residents of San Junipero is that the tourists are alive in their human bodies and travel to that dimension by coupling their bodies with a wearable device, whereas the residents have given up their human bodies and copied and pasted, so to speak, their consciousness and memories to external hardware.

The dream, or the risk, of the dematerialization of the body, imagined by the fiction of Black Mirror as by many others, is to be understood from the more general perspective of an ideology of transparency that responds to a desire for immediacy and exhibition, for which new technologies are a way to directly display and dispose of the world and of the body itself. In fact, screens have nowadays become interfaces through which we encounter the others and the world: a real world as well as a virtual one. In that role, screens increasingly work as bodily prostheses that enhance and extend human perception, knowledge, desire, and action. Indeed, the coupling of the body and screens has never been as evident as in recent decades, largely due to the diffusion of wearable devices and augmented reality technology. As has been pointed out by several studies, such a massive exteriorization of human capacities into technologies could, therefore, risk the dematerialization of bodily experience and even engender a progressive insensibilization of our perceptive, cognitive, and relational functions.

However, the actual use of wearable screens more often shows the reversal of that ideological design. In fact, wearable screens often operate by using bodily organs as prostheses. If bodily organs function as prostheses of screens, then those screens can be conceived as what Deleuze and Guattari call a "body without organs": an unstable, residual surface crossed by fluxes of desires, images, and data that disorganizes the hierarchy and transparency of the biotechnological organism. Thinking of the screen as a body without organs enables us to think of the screen within the libidinal body and its opacity, which invites the conceptualization of new forms of identities, desires, and memories that such disorganization provides.

8.1 Introduction

Spoiler alert! In an episode of the Netflix series *Black mirror*[1], a small device applied to the temple allows old people to take the forms of virtual figures – avatars that look like them when they were young –, and temporarily explore, as "tourists", a virtual *parallel dimension*. The place they go to – *San Junipero* – is a cyber-town, whose actual residents are not fictional characters, as they would be in a video game. San Junipero is not only a virtual reality, in fact, it is at the same time a massive database in the cloud where people's consciousness can be uploaded to, instead of dying. There is an *essential* difference, then, between the status of the latter, the *residents*, and the *tourists*, which are still alive in their human flesh: an almost invisible ontological gap that nevertheless structures in a very different way their experiences in the common space of San Junipero.

Once a week, on Saturday night, the tourists are travelling to the San Junipero-dimension as a form of therapy (or, most likely, as a form of promotion for their imminent after-life): the peculiar trip is possible thanks to the coupling of their bodies with a particular wearable device: the old and sick body (the temple, the brain, the eyes) is therefore used as a *screen* that projects and transports them into a young and functioning self, experiencing a sort of *embodied virtual simulation*[2]. The residents have given up their human bodies

---

[1] San Junipero, 4th episode of the 3rd season of the English Netflix series Black mirror, directed by O. Harris, written by C. Brooker, 61 minutes, releasing date the 21st October 2016.

[2] This expression, referring to the kind of virtual simulation experienced by the protagonists of *San Junipero (Black Mirror)*, interestingly evokes the Embodied Simulation Theory developed by Vittorio Gallese and Giacomo Rizzolati, for which "the fundamental mechanism that allows us a direct experiential grasp of the mind of others is not conceptual reasoning but direct simulation of the observed events through the mirror mechanism" [180]. A similar mechanism, called *Free Embodied Simulation* and which required the immobility of the body, is at the basis of our understanding of cinema and the moving image (cf. [75]; cf. also [76]). We have no elements to analyze the actual operation of the hypothetical technology used in this episode of Black Mirror, however,

instead, and "copied and pasted" their consciousness and memory to an external hardware, experiencing insofar a new digital form of life post-mortem, where the once called *soul*, and now called *mind*, can live beyond the existence of the human body, and yet still *embodied* both in a virtual, dematerialized body (the anthropomorphic avatar), and at the same time in a massive hard drive. The residents, therefore, inhabit the surface of an invisible *screen*, since the screen is the *umwelt* of an avatar and the connatural expressive space connected to a hard drive.

One familiar with our case study could object that – for once – there are no actual *screens* in this episode of *Black Mirror*. Which is true: the only screen in *San Junipero* is the one of our computer, tablet or smart television through which we're enjoying the show. But these latter are not secondary screens: in fact, there are no other ways to experience the virtual reality of San Junipero, to make it *visible*. Once in San Junipero, in fact, the protagonists of this episode are immersed in a virtual world that prevents them from seeing the screen they're inhabiting: that doesn't mean that there are no screens, but rather that they're on the screen, living on its surface. In order to make them believe in their experience, to make it more and more immersive, the screen must be invisible, because it's only when the screen is invisible that it can actually represent something. However, that's also why the screen, although denied and removed, is still present, also on a diegetic level. Its presence is, in fact, necessary to make this virtual world visible (and audible – screens are no longer separable from speakers), transforming the spectator into a witness, somehow part of the fiction itself because of its function; without witnesses, there's no San Junipero, no proof of this afterlife. The spectator is then indispensable to the dream of San Junipero and their inhabitants.

One could argue that the fact we're experiencing San Junipero through a screen doesn't mean that, in the dystrophic future described by this fiction, we'll still need to pass through a screen to join a virtual world. In other terms, one could argue that new technology won't need actual screens to make visible, audible and more generally liveable a virtual reality. However, we could also argue that throughout the last century, the constant proliferation and multiplication of screens have turned the screen into the optical, informational, computational and more generally existential *dispositive of reference* of

---

we'd like to suggest that the mechanism of *Embodied Simulation* (or *Free Embodied Simulation*, because of the status of immobility of patients while are experiencing the trip to San Junipero as therapy) could be a plausible description of the mechanism on which is based the mode of operation of this hypothetical technology.

our times. The screen has imposed itself as an unavoidable *metaphor*[3] for technology in general, for the whole process of mediation, with its possibility of regulating *regimes of light, regimes of enunciation*[4]. Therefore even when we're trying to go beyond the screen, as it might be in the case of *San Junipero*, the screen – even in its (apparent) absence – is still the referent of that effort, a silent metaphor, a functional model.

The metaphor isn't indeed the only figure of speech explaining the role of the *screen* in our times: we could say, paraphrasing *Stéphane Lojkine*[5], that the screen is also a metonymy: a part that stands for the whole process of mediation (*synecdoche*, a class of metonymy), an object for a more general technological function, a metaphor for a metamorphosis. It is in this double perspective then that we will think the role of the screen in *San Junipero*, as a metaphor and a metonymy of prosthetic technologies and embodied virtual simulations imagined by this fiction.

In this paper, we will eventually explore the reasons why this apparent absence of screens in *San Junipero* goes along with the paradoxical dematerialization of the body told by this story. But in order to do so, we'll have to understand in the first place the ideological nature of this dematerialization and, insofar, why this dematerialization tends to conceal the screen itself.

8.2 Part 1: The Ideology of Absolute Transparency

Platonism 2.0

The dream, or the risk, of a dematerialization of the body – drawn by this fiction as by many others – is to be understood in the more general perspective of an *ideology of absolute transparency*[6], which responds to a desire for immediacy and exhibition, according to which new technologies are a way to directly *dis-*

---

[3] Mauro Carbone defines the screen the optical dispositive of reference of our times in his Filosofia-schermi, [24]; cf. also [203, "The Scene of the Screen"]
[4] Cf. [36]
[5] Lojkine actually refers to the screen as a *metonymy* in the context of Theory of Literature, in order to develop "une modélisation dans l'espace qui passe par le primat de l'image sur le langage dans la production du sens, et de la prédétermination du sens par le dispositif spatial de son énonciation", cf. [111]
[6] Cf. M. Carbone, Les pouvoirs de l'archi-écran et de l'idéologie de la "transparence 2.0", talk in the International Conference Des pouvoirs des écrans, Lyon, the 23rd of September, video available at the following address:
https://www.youtube.com/watch?v=IcWKzCRwLVg
list=PLLtQXumaY4yu3CsNV7sEvU0iTSzPolheO index=4, last consultation 15/01/2018.

play, possess and dispose of the world and therefore of the body itself. According to this ideology then, new technologies should ensure the most immediate contact between the purest form of subjectivity and the reality, erasing as much as possible all traces of mediation in between: an apparently *naked truth* (for instance, reality reduced to data, perfect correspondence between the real and the virtual world, but also, just in apparent counter-tendency, fake news and post-truth) is given to the subject through almost transparent and systematic prostheses that make its organism more powerful. The dematerialization of the body operates then through a process of progressive transparency of the body itself and of its technological prostheses, which however doesn't imply a disorganisation of the body. On the contrary, a dematerialized body stays organic, systematic, as the most functioning and efficient organism.

In our view, the *ideology of absolute transparency* actually reveals itself as a 2.0 form of what Deleuze called Platonism [35], a simplified version of Plato's philosophy, which from Ancient Greece has become the dominant current in Western thought. When Friedrich Nietzsche claimed that "We no longer believe that truth remains truth when the veils are withdraw"[143:p8] and therefore that "Perhaps truth is a woman who has grounds for not showing her grounds"[7], he intended to overthrow the Platonism itself, for which – a *contrario* – the truth is rather conceived as a woman who has to show her grounds, to unveil herself. The *ideology of absolute transparency* evokes the mythical nudity of the truth, as well as the Platonism, except that here nudity is not unveiled but, precisely, seen in transparency, through transparency. It's this transparency that engenders the imperative of exhibition that identifies our times, the anthropological need and the desire to *see* as much as we can, as well as to *show* as much as we can, through the transparency of an almost invisible screen: a screen that exposes us, but at the same time shelters us, behind its transparent, concealed but unconsciously present surface (this function of *protection* is not available in the mythical nudity of Platonism). The *ideology of absolute transparency* transforms therefore the mythical nudity of Platonism in something obscene and almost pornographic, according to the general tendency of our times of radical exhibition, and consequent voyeurism: the truth is not revealed, but shamelessly displayed and – because of the obscenity of this exhibition – spied through a screen, in the very same way that pornography is compulsively consumed, hiding behind the very same screen. It's as if radical transparency was both the foundation of an ideology of absolute display of the truth (which is given to us without the dialectic between visible and invisible, showing and concealing, that characterized the

---

[7] Ibidem.

revelation of the truth [26:p20]), and of the compulsive need for obscenity that characterizes our times, of which the increasing consumption of online pornography is a symptom.

Representation, Remediation and Immediation

In a similar way, both Platonism and ideology of absolute transparency rely then on a logic of *representation*[8] for which the medium – therefore, today, the screen – has to be transparent and to connect our consciousness directly to the content it represents. The difference between the two is that, nowadays, the distance, the gap in between the subject and the object of representation must be as thin as possible, as transparent as possible, as imperceptible as possible. The ideology of transparency, insofar, brings the paradox of representation to its climax: a representation that is so transparent that doesn't believe in itself, in its function, anymore. In other terms, a representation that doesn't erase just the support of what is represented, but the gesture of representation itself.

The peculiar nature of this kind of representation is well described in Bolter and Grusin's *Remediation*[9], where what they call the double logic of immediacy and hyper-mediation explains how the desire for immediacy can be satisfied only through the complex architecture of hyper mediations, namely the proliferation of thin mediations that are so light that they can almost erase themselves, giving to the user the delusion of an immediate contact with reality, illusionary fulfilling its desire for immediacy. Remediation in itself is not a synonym of representation, but can be signified in a representative, dualistic – insofar Platonistic – way: in this case, mediation is a third, successive term placed in between two pre-existent ones, precisely the subject and the object of mediation itself, as Richard Grusin explains in *Radical mediation* [72].

The ideology of transparency displays then a politics of *immediation*, as "the seduction and the short-cuts of the great utopian figure of immediacy" [118], which operates through a denial of mediation itself. Immediation is then the *practical* and *therefore political* way through which ideology of transparency becomes real and effective, the means through which ideology displays itself [10]. We're facing the libidinal core of this ideology: the desire for immediacy is satisfied in an illusory way because of the denial of mediation itself. Transparency and immediacy are built then on a process of repression that involves the body as well, as the first and most immediate media-

---

[8] Cf. [115]
[9] [12], especially Introduction. The Double Logic of Remediation, pp. 2-19.

tion[10]. Understanding the dematerialization of the body through the *ideology of transparency*, through the politics of *immediation*, let us realize how the body is never really dematerialized, but just denied in its opacity, in its function of first, radical mediation: the dematerialization of the body implies then the denial of its prostheses and, more generally, of technologies, ensuring the process of mediation between the subjectivity and the world. We can insofar affirm that if the body is denied, the screen is denied as well.

8.3 Interlude: Symptomatology of Immediation

But what is denied doesn't disappear, but always returns – often under terrible forms. And, when it comes back, it comes back as a *symptom*. In the episode of *Black Mirror* we're analysing, we can find interesting symptoms following the dematerialization of the bodies and presented especially by the residents – those who instead of dying uploaded their *soul/mind* to the cloud and permanently live in San Junipero. Both visitors and residents, in fact, spend their nights in San Junipero going out to clubs, where they can listen and dance to the music of when they were young, drinking the same cocktails or wearing the same dresses – basically, reliving their youth over and over, and engaging in flirting/dating/sexual activities. While this perfectly satisfies the tourists, for the residents after a while, this is not enough anymore. They prefer attending a different club, a "club of excesses", where the drinking, dancing and flirting is replaced with sadomasochism, hard drugs and group sex, in order to push the enjoyment as far as possible, and of course, never succeeding in fulfilling it. This not only evokes the obscenity and pornographic imaginary behind the ideology of transparency, but it also stands as a symptom of the opposite and yet corresponding anaesthesia that characterises our times. An *anaesthesia* that becomes almost explicit during this episode when we repetitively see some residents jumping from a building or crashing with their cars just to desperately try to *feel something*. The dematerialization of the body – the denial of mediations – causes a loss of the *aesthetic* dimension of their experience, generating the urge to hurt themselves in order to feel something.

How should we interpret these symptoms? Jean-François Lyotard, in *Freud according with Cézanne*, and other contemporary essays collected in *Des dispositifs pulsionnels* [114], explained how the overthrow of the representative paradigm – that took place in Western culture at the end of XIX century, with Cézanne, artistic avant-gardes and, somehow, the birth of cinema – followed a *principle of derepresentation* that transformed our libidinal relation

---

[10] Cf. [71:p148]

with the work of art: instead of an illusory pleasure, the spectator – namely *beyond the pleasure principle*[11] – encounters the enjoinment itself, under the form of both sexual and death drives. The presence of death drives engenders what Lyotard qualifies as *desire for deception*. This turn is possible because the support of the work of art, the medium, or better the mediation itself, isn't invisible anymore, as it was in the representative paradigm, but it shows itself in the act of showing something. What are the effects of this opacity? In *Notes on the critical function of the work of art*, in order to describe what happens when the user, the spectator encounters the death drives, confronted through the opacity of mediation, Lyotard coins a meaningful expression: "se heurter à l'écran"[113:p238], to crash oneself onto the screen, and also to hurt oneself onto the screen. Thus, if the "club of excesses" – where the residents hang out desperately trying to beat boredom and the anaesthesia of their condition and to fulfil the imperative of enjoyment – tells us about this shift from the illusory satisfaction of pleasure to the excess of the enjoinment, the attempts of the residents of crashing their virtual bodies onto the screen goes even beyond, almost involuntarily evoking this expression of Lyotard, and showing the terrible form under which the opacity returns.

8.4 Part 2: The Resistance of Opacity

What we've been saying about San Junipero can be applied, with due differences, to our world and our experiences: enjoinment, violence, excesses, death drives, and at the same time a general anaesthesia, as well as the urge to crash ourselves onto the thin and almost invisible surface of the screen in order to feel something – and that something might be the screen itself –, all of these are aspects of our times that we're becoming more and more aware of. The first aim of this paper was then to read them under the symbolic influence of the ideology of absolute transparency, as effects of the *regime of light*[12] imposed by this ideology, of the denial of the opacity of mediation, conceived in its most *radical* sense (not only media, but also the body) [72:p148].

One other aim of this paper is then to elaborate a critique of this ideology of absolute transparency, a critique built starting from the symptoms of the return of opacity presented in our case study, a return that shows – in a more general way – an actual resistance of opacity to the ideology of absolute transparency, a resistance from the inside of this ideology. We shouldn't forget, in fact, that *transparency* itself indicates a particular degree of opacity: the

---

[11] Cf. [55]
[12] Cf. G. Deleuze, "What is a Dispositif?", op. cit., p. 168.

The Screen: a Body Without Organs

Latin etymology of this word show how it's composed by the prefix *trans*, that means *through*, and the suffix *pareo, to appear*. If transparency means then to *appear through*, already in its name it implies mediation, a *medium*, and therefore a connatural opacity. That's why speaking in terms of *absolute transparency* is already a linguistic and ontological paradox. In the second part of this paper, we will then try to philosophically explore the resistance of opacity to this paradox of an absolute transparency.

Technology and Default

Firstly, to account for the opacity of mediation, and insofar of the body, we need to re-signify the status of new technology as prosthesis of our body. With Bernard Stiegler's philosophy of technics, we can understand prosthesis not as an object or a tool added – in a secondary moment – to an organic and systematic body, that comes first; but rather as something that co-originates itself with the human being. Stiegler goes back to a tragic, pre-platonic way of thinking to technics, conceiving our ontological and libidinal relation to the technical object starting from the myth of Epimetheus and the key notion of *default*[13]. Instead of thinking the subject in the Platonistic way, as individual and organic but – therefore – lacking of something (lacking of the *object-cause* of its desire, as for instance the Psychoanalysis explains), Stiegler thinks the subjectivity along with the technical object itself: the default, differently from the lack, reveals the original technicity of the being of human beings and therefore marks their existence as indeterminacy, dispossession, non-closedness. In other words, the original technicity of human beings *projects* them outside of themselves. In his third volume on *Technics and Time*[14], Stiegler explains through the metaphor of cinema "the original exteriorization of consciousness as prosthetic projection" [89:p10], as well resumed by Eric Hörl in his *Prostheses of desire*. Prosthesis becomes then a sort of external consciousness, a centre of unification of the stream of consciousness: consciousness is not a pure (disembodied or dematerialized) entity that comes first and later uses the body and its prostheses as tools, but rather – as the metaphor of cinema shows – it's a process where the exteriorization and the projection are fundamental for the synthesis of the different fluxes of intensities. Insofar, Stiegler can qualify the screen as a *transcendental screen*: a surface of synchronisation of different intensities, and, at the same time, a plan of *dyachro-*

---

[13] Cf. [210]
[14] Cf. [211]

nisation of singularities. A plan of individuation, would say Simondon, of dividuations, we'd rather say with Mauro Carbone[15].

Prostheses: Organs Without Body

Thinking of prosthetic technologies, and insofar of prosthetic screens – technological prosthesis coupled in different ways with human body, in order to enhance bodily skills and performances – as co-originating with the human being, and not successive to it, that doesn't mean we must think of them in an organic and systematic relation with it – or with its body. On the contrary, we suggest that the dispossessive experience that the technical object produces inaugurates then the possibility of a radical disorganisation of the prostheses system and of the body as well. Insofar, technological prostheses, prosthetic screens can be thought of as *organs without bodies*, borrowing the formulation that Žižek takes and reverses from Deleuze and Guattari. We're jumping on the libidinal *pendant* of our co-originating relation with technological prostheses. According to Žižek re-interpretation of Deleuze, it's the disorganization of the organs – organs without an organism that control them – that lets the Real reveal itself through *talking objects* separated from a totalising and unifying body. The Real – in Lacan's terminology[16], recalled by Žižek – is precisely the dimension of our experience that is removed, repressed, denied, because of its limitless (and traumatic) libidinal nature: the core of our desires, what transcends every possible Symbolic representation, what cannot be represented[17]. This dimension is not available for the subject as such, since it's part of the Symbolic order of representation, but it's accessible for partial

---

[15] Cf. [24:p151-152].

[16] When Žižek refers to Real, he's addressing one of the three levels of our experience identified by Jacques Lacan, along with the Symbolic and the Imaginary. "For Lacan, the reality of human beings is constituted by three intertangled levels: the Symbolic, the Imaginary, and the Real. This triad can be nicely illustrated by the game of chess. The rules one has to follow in order to play it are its symbolic dimension: from the purely formal symbolic standpoint, 'knight' is defined only by the moves this figure can make. This level is clearly different from the imaginary one, namely the way in which different pieces are shaped and characterized by their names (king, queen, knight), and it is easy to envision a game with the same rules, but with a different imaginary, in which this figure would be called 'messenger' or 'runner' or whatever. Finally, real is the entire complex set of contingent circumstances that affect the course of the game: the intelligence of the players, the unpredictable intrusions that may disconcert one player or directly cut the game short", [230:p8-9]

[17] The Real has somehow a sublime nature: cf. the interpretation that Lyotard gives on the Kantian notion of sublime, as a negative presentation, a representation of the fact that there is something unrepresentable, in [113]

objects, disorganised organs, which with their libidinal surplus – and their ontological default – exceed the Symbolic dimension and enter the Real. This is how we should consider technological prostheses alternatively to the ideology of transparency: not as perfectly integrated and almost invisible limbs of our organism, but rather as *partial objects*, organs without a body.

What Žižek writes about cinema can be extended to the whole technological experience. Screens and cameras are then "casted eyes", partial objects "torn from the subject and freely thrown around"[229:p154]. This marks a discontinuity from the Platonism: the truth is not given through a speaking subject, but what remains of the truth, the Real, can be spoken by a partial object, a talking head, an autonomous prosthesis. No more is there a subject saying, "I Plato, am the truth"[142:p16], but an organ saying "it's me, the truth", where *me* marks a difference from *I* because of its a-subjective and partial nature. It's no longer the Heideggerian question of the *thrownness of being*, but merely the *thrownness of the eye*, and more generally of an organ. Where the *thrownness* outlines the residual nature of the organ in relation to the organism.

The Screen: A Body Without Organs

This radical autonomy of partial objects can engender then an interesting overthrow, following the overthrow of Platonism: screens – presented at first as technological prostheses of the body, both in a Platonistic and anti-Platonistic way (Stiegler and Žižek) – start using bodily organs – and the body as well, albeit a disorganised body – as prostheses, or *quasi-prostheses*[18] of themselves. Many wearable screens or wearable devices are already working in this way, using our bodies – or their organs – as a screen or, more generally, a prosthesis for their functioning[19]. As well as many biometric apps are doing, by making use of our bodies as they were computational and informational prostheses, functioning through the data they provide.

But if bodily organs function as prostheses of a screen, then that screen can be thought as what Deleuze and Guattari call a "body without organs", an unstable and residual surface crossed by fluxes of desires, images, data, disorganising the hierarchy and the transparency of the biotechnological organism. Thinking of the screen as a body without organs enables us to think of the screen within the libidinal body and its opacity, opening to an understanding of the new forms of identities, desires and memory that such *disorganisation* provides. In fact, a body without organs, for Deleuze and Guattari, is not a notion, a concept, but

---

[18] Cf. [24:p141-146].
[19] This is the case, for instance, of Google Glasses, cf. [129, Screens, p. 172]; cf. also [144]

rather a practice, a process through which the subject disposes of its subjectivity, of its organic totality. This is how we want to think the screen as a *quasi-subject*[20]: not a total screen [5, 8], but rather a screen that is denied, unconscious, thrown away, and yet resists as the residual and slippery surface of a body without organs, onto which intensities cannot fix themselves into individual identities. The screen as body without organs is then the residual and resisting element of the ideology of transparency: the opposite of the transparent screen that represents contents and refers to signifiers, transforming itself into a mirror where intensities can project themselves into fixed identities. As Deleuze and Guattari write, "A body without organs is made in such a way that it can be occupied, populated only by intensities. [35] Still, the BwO is not a scene, a place, or even a support upon which something comes to pass. It has nothing to do with phantasy, there is nothing to interpret" [35:p169]. The screen as a body without organs is a black mirror, it ceases to be the support of something, and it stands on its own: a screen (indirectly[21]) without images. Anything could transit on its surface, but nothing stays, nothing stands for something else, nothing can be signified. It's a transcendental screen of desire, a plan of immanence, where everything is virtually possible but not actualised.

This weird embodiment of the screen corresponds, therefore, to the becoming machine of the human being itself. That is the process through which, according to Deleuze and Guattari, the subject, following the model of the schizophrenic psyche, metamorphoses itself in an infinitely complex (and disorganised) machine, discovers its mechanical essence and gets rid of its individual subjectivity. In other terms, instead of asking ourselves if machines can imitate and emulate human mind or human affective and aesthetic experience, we should ask ourselves how the human mind, human emotions, feelings, sensations are actually built and depend on external machines, technologies, mediations. The libidinal process of becoming machine shows, once again, the mutual origin of human being and technical object, of human being and machines, and therefore their co-dependence.

That is, after all, the sense of what Grusin calls a *radical mediation*, and what makes mediation a part of the ontogenetic process. The materiality of mediation and its technological components are not simply secondary aspects but essential parts of the process of mediation itself. Mediation, here, is not a third element that comes after subject and reality, but is co-originating with them. Everything, human beings and technological realities, transform themselves together within the process of mediation. Insofar, as Grusin claims, "human body

---

[20] Cf. [24:p122-126].
[21] A black mirror presents images only in an negative way, cf. [114:p150]

is a radically nonhuman mediations among other nonhuman mediations" [72:p148]. That is the resistance of opacity, the becoming machine of the body and this peculiar embodiment of the screen, as a body without organs. That is the opaque face of politics of *immediation* [10] that demands to be explored, to think what stays marginal in the contemporary society of absolute transparency.

Chapter 9

Techno-Aesthetics and Technics of the Body From Merleau-Ponty to Simondon and Back

Anna Caterina Dalmasso

Centre Prospéro. Langage, image et connaissance
Université Saint Louis – Bruxelles

Summary

In his account of technics, Leroi–Gourhan makes no essential distinction between the tool as a technical organ and the organ as a bodily element. A technical object —a biface, for example—emerges from the sensible matter in the same way as the hand insofar as they both are a "secretion of the body and the brain" and entail a "technique of the body". In fact, technological tools and devices should never be considered in isolation, because they exist only in relation to the interminglings between bodies and society that they make possible or that make them possible.

Thus, technicity, understood in its broadest sense as exteriorization, cannot be thought of as something that is merely added to a so-called "natural" core of embodied life but in its mutual implication with sensibility, that is, in its relationship with the development and historical evolution of the living body understood—in its inseparable connection with the mind— as the junction between the sensible and the symbolic, the organic and the cultural, and perception and expression.

In this paper, I investigate the reciprocal implications of embodied aesthetic thinking and technical thinking in order to show how technicity, as a cultural and symbolic attitude, is rooted in the aesthetic dimension of human experience, understood not only as the relationship to artistic creation but more radically as the human body's ability to aesthetically engage with the world. In a complementary way, I examine the sensible genesis of the living body's technicity and address the decisive question of how technics can inflect and catalyze changes in the human sensorium, thinking, and intersubjective relationships.

My contribution articulates these questions in the wake of Merleau–Ponty's phenomenology of the body, especially with regard to the connection between the living body's motricity and symbolism, and on the basis of Simondon's groundbreaking reflection on technics, particularly his conception of techno-aesthetics—that is, a primitive form of our contact with the world or of technics in its functional aspects—to develop a cross-reading of the theoretical account of the body and technics made by the two philosophers.

9.1 Introduction

Because of the increasingly pervasive presence of technology in our lives, the question of technics, and especially that of its relationship to sensibility, has become crucial under many respects. Technological devices, as well as the cultural and epistemological dispositives – in a Foucaultian sense – they set out, work as a prosthesis of human sensibility and expand the capacities of the intersubjective sphere, entailing political and biopolitical issues and affecting our embodied existences.

In order to address such questions in a comprehensive perspective, contemporary studies have frequently turned to the ground-breaking reflection developed by Gilbert Simondon, providing a wide account of technicity and of its longtime neglected cultural significance ([198] MEOT). In this paper, I would like to challenge Simondon's fascinating perspective through a cross-reading between his work on technicity and Merleau-Ponty's reflection on the phenomenal body ([122] *Phénoménologie de la perception* hereafter Php; [126] *Le monde sensible et le monde de l'expression* hereafter MSME)

Certainly, Merleau-Ponty is not known for having developed a systematic account of technics, nevertheless, as some contributions have tried to show [94, 73, 74, 77], it is possible to identify some elements in his philosophy that allow us to sketch out if not an organic reflection on technics at least a set of very productive and operational concepts to think of it.

The goal of this paper is not just to highlight points of contact between Merleau-Ponty's thought and Simondon's, which are many, but rather to reciprocally shed light on the conception of technics developed by the two philosophers and, by combining their works, try to encompass their internal limits. By emphasizing significant points of convergence, I intend, on the one hand, to show how Simondon's philosophy comes to develop some insights brought forward by Merleau-Ponty's reflection, and, on the other hand, to push further Simondon's conception through Merleau-Ponty's account of the living body's technicity.

In order to prevent any misleading interpretation, I would like to make it clear that, by setting out this comparison, I do not aim to make Merleau-Ponty a philosopher of technology. On the contrary, I prefer to stress what motivates this apparently arbitrary choice, namely the fact that, if nowadays we come to address a phenomenology of the body in search for the elements for a theory of technicity, this reveals how our present historical situation urges us to consider the connection between sensibility and technics, as it gains special value in the perspective of contemporary technoculture.

9.2 Technics and culture

If we examine Merleau-Ponty's approach of technics, it may appear ambivalent: on the one hand, the philosopher strongly opposes a *technicization* of thought [74], that is a causalist way of thinking, but, on the other hand, he takes technology into consideration as non-philosophical field, whose symbolic and cultural significance calls for a philosophical investigation and opens new paths for philosophy.

In *The Structure of Behaviour*, we find a number of examples and metaphors drawn from the technical domain, that support Merleau-Ponty's claims against a mechanicist conception of thought and science. Nevertheless, more often, Merleau-Ponty's argument relies upon phenomenological descriptions of technical dispositives, read as correlatives of the configuration of the human body and its excessive structure: the analysis of technical artefacts is set forth so as to reveal the bodily perceptive structures that are normally dissimulated and remains unnoticed in our everyday life. Thus, it is worth noting that in this argumentative approach technology acts as a revealing of the very functioning of sensibility[1]. So, although Merleau-Ponty argues against a technicization of thought, his main philosophical argument seems to pursue another direction of research that could be schematized in the next points:

1) Merleau-Ponty *refuses the nature/culture opposition*. The French philosopher refuses the idea of nature as a separate entity, and he rather aims to demonstrate that "what we call nature is already consciousness of nature" ([121, SC:199,SB:184] *La structure du comportement* hereafter SC, its English translation, *The Structure of Behavior hereafter* SB.). Nature is not behind us as an unreachable dimension that we could eventually access if we could get

---

[1] This argument is developed for instance in particular in the famous Merleau-Ponty's conference on cinema, see [123:p48-59]

"beyond" culture. Rather, nature is the background on which the human being lives and is the source of the excess of meaning and sense characterizing human nature. As Merleau-Ponty writes, what characterizes the human being is "not the capacity to create a second nature – economic, social or cultural – beyond biological nature; it is rather the possibility to overcome these given structures for creating new ones"[2].

2) This is particularly remarkable with regard to the movement of *dilatation* of *perception* (M. Merleau-Ponty's *Le visible et l'invisible* hereafter VI. [124, fr:262,en:212]) which is afoot in our embodied relationship to technical objects. Indeed, what enables our relationship to instruments and technologies is the *virtual power of the body image or body schema*[3] – supporting the living body's memory, spatiality and motility, which is experienced proprioceptively and dynamically and through which the phenomenal body is geared onto the world – to be understood as a theoretical framework for our relationship to technicity.

As the American post-phenomenologist Don Ihde has pointed out, Merleau-Ponty's account of body image is implicitly a theory of the process of technical exteriorization and incorporation or, as he puts it, a "latent phenomenology of instrumentation" [94:p40]. For, in Merleau-Ponty's view, the body image has the power of "dilating our being-in-the-world" and "changing our existence by appropriating instruments" (PhP 168 / 127).

By virtue of the virtual power of the body image, even before being involved in action and movement, the living body is already engaged in the virtual projection of them. For, the body image does not only present us immediately with our bodily position and proprioception but offers a system which is open on to the world and creatively integrates and realigns to it.

Thus, the way we get used to technical objects and artifacts – such as the feather of a hat, a car, or a white cane for a blind person (See PhP 167 / 128) – is to be transplanted into them, or conversely, to incorporate them into the bulk of our own body. In their relationship with human sensibility, things cease to be mere objects and become instead "quasi-organs" [191:p107],

---

[2] SC 189 / SB 175 (modified translation).
[3] "Body image" is the expression Paul Schilder uses in his major work which is one of the more important Merleau-Ponty's sources on this topic [193]. If Merleau-Ponty seems to prefer the term "schéma" this is because he tends to follow Head's and Lhermitte's vocabulary. Still, he claims that the body image theory needs a new method to be deeply understood, and he intends to re-elaborate such a concept. See [122:p113] hereafter PhP. About these questions see [191].

contributing to our being open to the world and realizing an "extension of existence" (PhP 178 / 135).

3) In fact, technics produces a symbolic and cultural projection or excess of our "natural" embodied and adaptive actions; in this sense, technical objects can be considered an "expression" just as, for Merleau-Ponty, perception is in itself expressive, insofar as it expresses the human being by expressing things (MSME, 48).

This brings us to the third point I wanted to highlight: the *need for a philosophical investigation of the cultural meaning of technology*. For Merleau-Ponty, philosophy needs to investigate technologies and more in general technical objects as anthropological facts able to revive and put into question philosophical reflection.

As he claims in his Collège de France 1958 courses [125], the advancement of technology and the development of modern physics – in the same way as modern art, and contemporary literature and cinema – *are a permanent call to philosophy and its renewal*.

9.3 Technical culture and aesthetic thinking

Thus, Merleau-Ponty sees in the manifestations of technics a sort of "unthought", with which philosophy must reckon. Such a direction of research has been taken on and pursued by Gilbert Simondon, in particular by his reflection on the mode of existence of technical objects.

In his approach of technicity, Simondon's goal is precisely to bring out the cultural significance of technics and to raise awareness of the meaning of technical objects, that our culture seems to have denied, refusing technical realities as essentially human (See MEOT, 9, translation mine). By neglecting the meaning and human genesis of technical objects, the established theory has ended up drawing an opposition between the human being and the machine; this has prevented from considering technical objects as "mediators between human being and nature" (MEOT, 9 translation mine[4]).

Interestingly, in Simondon's view, the potential of the technical sphere hinges on the aesthetic dimension, in which resides its virtual possibilities. In the third part of his book *On the Mode of Existence of Technical Objects*, the philosopher develops a symbolic history of the three different modes of being-in-the-world

---

[4] See also: "There are in fact three types of reality: the world, the subject and the intermediary object between the world and the subject, whose first form is that of the technical object", MEOT, 170 (translation mine).

of the human – *magical phase, religious phase, technical phase* –, to be thought of as successive individuations of a metastable system.[5] In the first mode of existence, the relation of the human being to the world comes about in an elementary structuration, which precedes the separation between subject and object. The human being experiences a primitive unity with the world in which emerges a "reticulation" of points instituting salient moments and places functioning as "key-points" (MEOT, 229) and polarities.

The constitution of the technical phase and of the religious phase proceeds from the rupture of this initial structure: resulting in a phase-shift [*déphasage*] of the primitive magical mode of existence. The unity of the living being and its environment is divided and it becomes, on the one hand, objectivated by technics and, on the other hand, subjectivated by religion.

Now, with respect to the results of this phase-shift, the *aesthetic thought* acts for Simondon as "a permanent reminder of the rupture of the unity of the magical mode of existence and the striving for future unity" (MEOT, 160, translation mine). What the philosopher names the "aesthetic thought" is what opens the possibility of reconstituting a reticular universe where humans directly experienced the world without separation between subject and object – that is, as they did in the magical phase. From this perspective, every aesthetic action consists in constituting noteworthy and salient points, by inserting it in the environment, issued from the phase shift of the magical world in the technical world and in the religious world.

By virtue of these elements, Simondon's reflection on technics offers an original framework to undo the opposition that can be established between the technical environment and the natural world, the process of *insertion* providing and implying the possibility of a *permanent reactivation of the critical and symbolic functions in the associated milieu.*

Simondon claims that aesthetic impression is independent of the real presence of an aesthetic object and can embrace every human experience (See MEOT, 249). Technical objects can have aesthetic value and can be said to be beautiful, not just because of the decoration or the shape they are provided with, but precisely by virtue of their intrinsic technicality (See MEOT, 254), since, for Simondon, aesthetic impression originates from the very action or process of insertion of the object in an environment.

Simondon's approach then does not directly take into account our bodily engagement to technical objects, but nonetheless intimately connects

---

[5] See also [200]

technicity to the aesthetic thought, as these two dimensions of existence cannot be separated.

9.4 Techno-Aesthetics and Technics of the Body

Later in his reflection, Simondon will outline the theoretical core of the intimate connection between technics and aesthetics, by introducing the notion of *techno-aesthetics* ([199] *Sur la technique* hereafter: STE, 380 / *On Techno-Aesthetics*: OTA). Technical objects – such as the Tour Eiffel, the Garabit viaduct, but also the engine of an automobile or the specific arrangement of a clamp, a shear, a stepped key and so on – can raise an aesthetic or techno-aesthetic impression: the first ones by virtue of their insertion in the geographic environment, with which they re-establish a unity, while machines or instruments can elicit an aesthetic feeling which does not derive from the contemplation of their insertion in the world, but *from the action* connected to them, i.e. since their use triggers a "sensorimotoric pleasure" or "pleasure of action" (STE, 383 / OTA).

Furthermore, by claiming that "no object is indifferent to our aesthetic need" (STE, 384-85 / OTA), the philosopher introduces a "more primitive, more fully physical sense" of techno-aesthetics (STE, 386 / OTA), as what inflects our practices and our choices, operating at a very deep level, the one that is often exploited by commercial strategies[6]. Indeed, aesthetics understood as *aisthèsis*, affects and determines the whole spectrum of our behavior: "The *aisthèsis*, the fundamental perceptive intuition, is part of a culture. It acts like a pre-selector, separating the acceptable from the unacceptable, and determining whether one will accept or refuse" (STE, 387 / OTA).

Aesthetics and technics shall not be considered separately, rather, between these two dimensions there is an "intercategorial fusion". As Simondon writes: "The techno-aesthetic feeling seems to be a category that is more primitive than the aesthetic feeling alone, or than the technical aspect considered from the angle of functionality alone (which is an impoverishing perspective)." (STE, 391-392 / OTA emphasis mine)

Here we find a crucial point of intersection between Simondon's reflection and Merleau-Ponty's conception of the connection between technicity and sensibility. As we have seen before, for Merleau-Ponty technics is the expression of the virtuality of the human body, of its capacity to extend and project itself into embodied significations. What the philosopher highlights is that

---

[6] See Simondon's insightful remarks about the observations of the *Food Research Institute* in India, STE, 387 / OTA

technicity is inscribed in the phenomenal body or we could say – in his later terminology – in the flesh, as amplification and emanation of the structure of the human *aisthésis*, and more specifically, of the constitutive gap in the sensible as the texture of differentiation.

This is particularly striking if we consider the example of the mirror that Merleau-Ponty evokes in a passage from *Eye and Mind* describing the reflective surface as what, on the one hand, incorporates a natural technicity, and, on the other, enacts, by virtue of a repetition of the natural world, the perceptive and imaginative capacity of the human being. But, it is only in connection with the reflexivity of the sensible that we can understand the reflexivity of the mirror.[7]

Thus, the mirror can be interpreted as the emblem of technics as radical exteriorization, as a projection of the human into the inorganic – in the same way as prosthesis, instruments, dispositives, etc. – but also into the organic – from the pseudopodium developed by the amoeba, to the most complex biological structures.

At the same time, borrowing Simondon's terms and sketching out a convergence with Merleau-Ponty's perspective, the mirror could be said to perform a techno-aesthetic function, as long as it institutes a salient and noteworthy point, which *allows the unification between nature and the human being as well as between my proprioceptive sensibility and the visual surface of my own body*. According to Merleau-Ponty, the mirror is inscribed in the flesh as much as it "draws my flesh outside" (OE 33 / EM 359). Any technique is already inscribed in my flesh – is a "technique of the body" [8] in Marcel Mauss' terms – by virtue of its originary alteration.

Therefore, if we read Simondon in the prism of Merleau-Ponty's account of technics, we can even push further his conception of techno-aesthetics by extending it to the very structure of the human body, of technics *in the flesh*.

In fact, Merleau-Ponty speaks of the body itself as the fundamental medium of our being open to the world, as a "machine for living the world", and – in the wake of Mauss' work and of a tradition that will be pursued by Leroi-Gourhan in the domain of ethnography and anthropology – of our eyes and our hands as a "technique", not in the sense of an objectified instrument, but as the virtual power that is inscribed in human sensibility.

---

[7] Merleau-Ponty's *L'œil et l'esprit* hereafter: OE, its English translation *Eye and Mind*: EM, [124, OE:33, EM:359]. About the mirror in Merleau-Ponty see [40:p63] and [191]

[8] Merleau-Ponty implicitly refers to Marcel Mauss's 1936 essay [117]

In this perspective, technics is not the product of culture over nature, but rather the expression of a permanent or radical mediation between the sensible and the symbolic operated in an embodied and carnal existence, so inscribing technics in our carnal being – at the same time carnal *and* technical.

So, if Simondon articulates the question of an originarity of technics not as an isolated anthropological or transcendental character, but as it is inseparable from the structure of human sensibility – originarity of the techno-aesthetic feeling – then Merleau-Ponty's reflection converges with Simondon's in the effort of thinking together the aesthetic dimension and the technical, but, in a more radical way, the author of *Eye and Mind* shows how technicity hinges on and institutes itself in the very structure of the flesh.

Thus, what can be considered to be original is not just human instrumentality or the act of delegating functions to technical objects or machines, but rather the ontological gap and internal alteration that is inscribed in the flesh, with respect to which technicity is an amplification, a further articulation, both natural and cultural.

Part IV - Applications of Philosophy on Technology

Chapter 10

Essays on Applications of Philosophy on Technology

What does "The Real Housewives of Hungary" teach about the philosophy of technology?

Eszter Nádasi

- Why did you drive your car when it is a self-driving one?
- Because when it drives itself (...) I am afraid.
- You should have to sit in the backseat and let it drive.
- It does not work like that, it is not that clever.

This quote from the Hungarian version of "The Real Housewives" (created by Viasat3) is an example on how popular culture informs television viewers about the potentials of innovative technologies such as the self-driving car (in this case, a Tesla). On the other hand, the reality show confronts them with a significant standpoint according to which it is not a rational choice to manually drive a self-driving model. Furthermore, the show presents the social context in which this car is embedded: since the characters of the series are so-called "luxury wives" – rich, married women – it is clear that the Tesla is a status symbol: to own and operate a Tesla is a privilege of wealthy citizens.

As this example shows, in general, our environment does not encourage us to use our own skills when easily replaceable with technological developments. Consider the following examples:

1. The calculator: is it not worth to use our mind and memory if the activity that we intend to perform can be automatic? There are activities that were regarded as the topgallants of human activities (for instance chess, data organization, math-

ematical calculation), but as it turned out these activities are the easiest to make automatic. Calculators are faster, more reliable and more precise than mental arithmetic, so people tend to spare themselves from calculating. The educational system not necessarily rewards those students who try to use their head or a paper and pen instead of the calculator: because it is more time consuming to calculate without the machine, thus the student will be behind the class. Except if (s)he has a special talent for calculation. It is only rational to not use the calculator if you can work as fast as the machine. But in general, we tend not to believe that someone is capable of doing the same mathematical calculation as effectively as the machine. Furthermore, people with special talent are usually regarded as geniuses – and their status is also commonly medicalized (by connecting the special talent to psychiatric dysfunctions). So, the bigger cognitive effort is not a rewarding activity in itself, the school rather trains the students to replace their efforts with machines, if machines are available for the given activities; and it also encourages them to focus on the tempo of their activity and success. The message is that you should simplify and reduce some activities by the application of technology in order to be successful.

2. The dishwasher: the manual completion of repetitive, reproductive, economically not directly profitable activities utterly seems irrational. Consider the following sentences:

   - "I like to do the washing up, so I will not buy a washing machine."

   - "I have a washing machine, but from time to time I do the washing up."

   - "I have a washing machine, but I like to do the washing up, because it is relaxing, so from time to time, I do it."

Housekeeping activities are usually considered to have a lower status; these are neither fancy forms of relaxation, nor activities that are capable of creating flow.

When home appliances were not as developed and well-designed as today, it might have seemed more rational to work manually instead of using these devices. For instance, when food mixers were big, heavy and hard to clean, people were more likely to work manually – using knives and shredders for instance – because it took a considerable amount of time to set up and maintain the machine. The difficulty of using these food mixers likely encourages developers to create more practical and ergonomic models.

If we look around in our houses, how many objects and machines will we find that are nice to have, but not truly necessary for everyday life? In this category, I put the case of the fondue maker that I got from my friends: before having it I never ever thought about purchasing one, but since I've had it, I have one more option for preparing food. Regular usage of such devices easily leads to a routine – more and more technologies thus become integral parts of our everyday life.

It is worth considering whether the use of technology adds to the value of our work-related or everyday activities, or, on the contrary, it takes away from it. As one of the studies in this chapter points out, the idea that Renaissance and later artists used tools – such as different lenses to make their drawings and paintings – have given some controversial reputation. Should a work of art be less precious if someone can convincingly testify the use of these tools? Well, as it seems, probably.

Today it is widely accepted to use various gadgets for creating art; however, the ownership of these technologies does not make us artists. Think about the flood of Photoshopped pictures on Instagram that are full with special effects – how many of these pictures have real aesthetical value? Of course, the question aesthetical hierarchy, the status of artifacts and taste is a big factor in this case, because these have a considerable role in the division between the so-called high and low quality creations. Carbon papers were widely used to copy hand-written documents and these also helped kids to copy draws. These kinds of drawings never had an artistic value; on the other hand, these papers might help to improve their manual skills. Similarly, black lines help to shape handwriting. Thus these special papers are often used in primary school education. However, students are expected to leave this technology behind after a certain amount of time and write in well organized lines without it.

Good technology is not enough to create an artist, but in many cases, innovative machines and programs (for instance cameras and software for cutting) can generate a competitive edge among artists. Furthermore, today the usage of different technologies does not query the state of being artists or artifacts.

10.1 Who controls whom?

In summary, people are users of technology by necessity. Today, in the age of "intelligent" technologies it is not only an option to use the developments, but it is an expectation as well. According to a technological determinist point of view, technology plays a governing force in our everyday life and people are locked-in in their technological environment since they have a certain set of devices (of course, people in different cultures may have somewhat different sets). As the studies in the chapter show, this locked-in situation existed in earlier historical periods as well, and the future user of the self driving car will experience it too. Nowadays, in order to be effective, precise and high standard professionals, also need to be digitally literate and we need to understand different theories in the philosophy of technology, as one of the studies states.

So, for what we are saving and using our cognitive capacities and manual skills in the time of intelligent machines? For those activities that are not replaceable by technological tools, and to retrieve the technology-created damages and side effects (externalities). Beyond the reduction of damages, we intend to make technological improvements and make the already existing and forthcoming technologies safer, in order to prevent future problems. These issues are addressed in the chapter by analyzing the Hillary Clinton email scandal from the perspective of crisis communication. As the given study shows, technology is not only a source of crisis, but a solution for these as well.

Control of technology is a key activity today: people invest a considerable amount of energy in the management of "self-functioning" machines and processes. The concept of control has a key role in the four articles of the section, according to the authors' indication:

1. the use of technology helps to control the relationship of a painting or drawing to the reality. Controlled and conscious use of different tools enable the artist to create verisimilitude;

2. technology allows professionals to control and prevent crisis situations;

3. it is worth considering a case in which people voluntarily give up their control of technology - as in the case of the self-driving car;

4. there are situations in which people partially delegate their decision-making processes to decision-support systems.

All of these articles show in different ways how technology is capable of serving, helping, supplementing or even replacing us – whether we talk about everyday activities like driving, decision making in various fields of life, in case of crisis or creative work.

The authors explain concepts from the field of philosophy of science that help to clarify the development and usage of technology and its interaction with individuals and society as a whole. As they show, occurrences in the past, present and potential future are worth considering from a technology-centered point of view. The authors analyze topically relevant events and problems with philosophical tools and they tend to apply Borgmann's concepts (device paradigm, focal things, postmodernism and hyperreality). The books of the German-born American philosopher of technology, Albert Borgmann are a reference point in these articles (for example: "Technology and the Character of Contemporary Life"; "Crossing the Postmodern Divide"; "Real American Ethics").

10.2 A short introduction of the articles

Alexandra Karakas: "Did Mirrors Determine Caravaggio?"

In 2010, the British painter David Hockney and the physicist Charles Falco made a controversial claim in their book "Secret Knowledge – Rediscovering the Lost Techniques of the Old Masters". According to them, artists like Caravaggio used various lenses and mirrors for their drawings and paintings and because of this the vividness and verisimilitude of their pictures improved considerably.

As the author of this study states, this account is a technological determinist interpretation of their work. On the other hand, art historians tend to explain the change in the former painting style from within their own discipline. They fail to consider the technological progress as a fundamental moving force shaping this phenomenon. Karakas provides historical overviews and background stories for her work and provides interesting facts about visual arts and technological developments of this field; further she presents several arguments from the field of art history. According to her study, decisions of the artists – for instance regarding their style – and the verisimilitude of their work are considerably influenced by their technological opportunities.

Peter Neuman and Daniel Gergo Pinter: "Technology-based Critical Phenomena - A Borgmannian Approach to Crisis Prediction"

"The crisis management professional needs to be able to predict crises in their everyday practice" – Neuman and Pintér contend. But how is that possible? With an application of Albert Borgmann's device paradigm, the authors of this article propose a new method for communication management professionals that can predict and even avoid crisis; furthermore, they aim to show an example of the practical relevance of Borgmann's theories for philosophers of technology. They aim to promote an understanding of those crises that emerge as a negative consequence of technological progress – for this; the authors provide a definition and classification of crisis situations. They use the controversial case of the Hillary Clinton email as a case study in this article.

Balázs Horváth: "Nudging for Hyperreality - A Philosophical Study of Technological Choice Architecture"

"Opting for no control" – this is the title of the thought experiment proposed by Horváth who aims to connect Borgmann's philosophy of technology with the nudge theory of economical decision making as it was published by Richard H. Thaler and Cass Sustein in 2008. According to the argument, the wide accessibility of driverless cars will present an opportunity to more deeply enter a state of hyperreality for the users of this technology. Seemingly, this innovative tool will provide more options for the users, but in reality, their choices will be limited, because the demand for comfort will reduce the number of opportunities. The author predicts the widespread and taken-for-granted usage of the self-driving function: drivers thus will opt for the experience of technological hyperreality, instead of manual driving.

Ákos Gyarmathy: "The Problem of Undermined Evidence – Accurate Entitlement for Epistemic Systems in Automatic Decision Support Systems"

The first chapters of this article introduce the operation of decision support systems – that are particularly popular in Medicine – and provide a brief history of the concept. Following these, the author elaborates an epistemological problem, namely the case of the uncertain inputs. Nowadays, the reasoning of decision support systems usually relies on the so-called classic Bayesian framework that is based on the certainty of the evidence. However, this certainty is an ideal and a rare situation. Thus Gyarmathy suggests the application of Jeffrey's conditionalization that can calculate with uncertain evidence instead of the prevailing one. By comparing the mathematical models of conditional probability, the author formalizes the current problems of a decision-making system and aims to make progress in their treatment.

10.3 Back to popular culture

Ákos Gyarmathy's study brings the perspective of Medicine into this chapter, and this field of science can be connected to a genre of popular culture that is so popular as reality shows which were discussed briefly at the beginning of this Introduction. Medical drama series tend to miss the opportunity to introduce the operation of decision-support systems that are used in some fields of Medicine with great success. Instead, these shows tend to represent the diagnostic process as a miraculous event: usually an individual medical superhero suddenly realizes the illness of the patient. In the case of House, this process usually happens in an office, for the process a white board and some pens are used. The medical team is responsible for making the examinations that are ordered by their boss, and option after option is dropped from the selection of potential diseases. This is not mere guessing or a series of opportunistic experiments on the patients, but the conscious reasoning process of professionals is usually not displayed in this popular genre. However, these series would have been a good source to make decision-support systems and the potential controversies around them understandable for the lay audience – just as "The Real Housewives" is capable of raising important issues about self-driving cars.

Chapter 11

Did Mirrors Determine Caravaggio?

Alexandra Karakas

Budapest University of Technology and Economics

Summary

Around the 15th century, a sudden change happened in painting regarding vividness and verisimilitude. Traditionally, art history explains this phenomenon within the discipline and does not consider technological progress fundamental. In my paper, I present briefly what David Hockney and Charles Falco stated about this question, and then explain my interpretation of their thesis. I argue that their claim about why paintings changed is a type of technological determinist theory and that the topic connects as much to the philosophy of technology as to art history. Within this, I point out that because of the usage of specific technological devices, like *camera obscura, camera lucida*, and different lenses some internal explanations of artistic expressions are no longer available in the discourse of mainstream art history. I use the Hockney-Falco thesis as a case study to support a determinist reading of art history dominated by technological devices. These statements imply that, from a technological determinist point of view, yet hidden layers of art history could be revealed, and because of this, we need to rethink certain assumptions regarding artistic decisions for instance.

11.1 The Hockney-Falco thesis and its context

David Hockney, the British painter, and Charles Falco, a physicist and professor at the University of Arizona published their rather controversial book *Secret Knowledge: Rediscovering the Lost Techniques of the Old Masters* in 2001 [88]. What they claimed is that artists like Caravaggio or van Eyck used concave mirrors and different lenses when making a picture, let it be painting or drawing, as early as the beginning of the Renaissance – three hundred years before art historians suspected it – to project parts of the images illuminated mainly by sunlight onto a canvas or board. When artists were working on a picture, they had to copy these projected images and bring together the small parts of it. They claimed that this phenomenon, the use of these devices was the cause of the considerable improvement regarding vividness and verisimilitude which influenced the visual canon as well. According to their thesis, lenses and mirrors, so different technological devices could help artists solve problems like the accuracy of the perspective, the correctness of lights on paintings, or the problem of how can complex three-dimensional objects be presented on a two-dimensional surface. The first problem which connects to all the issues is the problem of perspective. Hockney's and Falco's empirical method when testing out the task of reproducing three-dimensional images onto two-dimensional surfaces was that they merely compared a lot of images, and they were giving an account of the actual process of making [38:p147]. In some cases, they recreated specific scenes to demonstrate their thesis [33:p134].

Back then this was a controversial statement: the thesis has been attacked from a lot of different fields: after the book was published there was even a conference where critics and art historians responded to the book and mainly criticized it. They considered as a cheat if the artist used optical devices and took Hockney's interpretation as an attack against art itself, which would destroy the idealistic ethos around art and artists [38:p143]. Although Hockney and Falco have a new, different answer to this than the usual ideas, in their opinion the use of these devices was not cheating nor that it would destroy the romantic ethos of art history. According to them, what happened is not that artists suddenly could draw better nor that they looked at the word in a new way because of some philosophical transformation in their mind suddenly for no reason. Instead, what happened was caused by technological devices, but this claim does not mean some deskilling. 'Optics do not make art. The lens, the mirror, and the camera obscura are all just tools. The point is that artists encountered them much earlier than anyone thought' [20], claimed Hockney. Also, art historians, on the one hand, noted the lack of argumentation on previous works of the relation between artists and specific devices, and on the other hand, were concerned about the technical account of the actual process [65:p296]. Even though historians and art historians do not know much about how artists worked if there was a live model there during the whole process, or how much they redesigned the final piece [64].

11.2 Why technological determinism?

What Hockney and Falco did not discuss is the determinist reading of their interpretation from a technological point of view. The reason why I claim that this is a question at least as much of technology as of art theory is because what lead these processes within art history are the technological devices. Thus the improvement verisimilitude wise was caused by particular tools. When using a *camera lucida* for instance, which is a convex piece of glass on a stand, while drawing there is the device, through which the artist sees the setting she wants to copy, and also the paper, and on it the scene and her hand as well. Thus, the artist was only able to see the image through some device. This helped to master the famous Renaissance perspective, with which artists could give three-dimensional depth to their work by having a linear perspective, horizon line, and vanishing point as well. The greatest advantage of the *camera lucida* was that one could have used it in daylight, not like in the case of *camera obscura* where an image is projected through a small hole into a dark room or a box onto a surface. In this case, the image is inverted and reversed. That way it was a lot harder to copy the projected scenes than with *camera lucida*.

Naturally, there is always within every artwork a tool that has been used, which on the one hand, formed the piece, and on the other hand became part of it in some way. In contemporary art, for instance, it is easier to spot this phenomenon: whether it be a printer that produced a picture or a video camera that recorded an event or even a movie, in most of the cases devices are inseparable from the actual artwork. Although these seem to be a bit trivial, there are other cases in traditional art history where the role of particular technological devices has not been clarified yet. This was the case with the aforementioned question of art history, namely that what happened around the 15th century, why painters suddenly made better pictures regarding vividness and verisimilitude, and what other consequences appeared at the same time? Thus, the influences of these devices have been discussed insufficiently by Hockney and Falco, mainly because the technological perspective is not as elaborate and fine-grained as the one pertaining to art history, even though the latter effects were caused by the aforementioned devices.

My interpretation is based on technological determinism, which is part of a bunch of determinist theories. Although the term technological determinism is more common than autonomous technology, their meaning is intertwined and related. As with everything, there are a lot of definitions of what technological determinism is, but the primary argument shared by all types of theories is that technology is the governing force that shapes and leads society in a certain direction. On the other hand, autonomous technology as a term refers to the thesis that 'technology is not in human control, that it develops with a logic of its own' [41:p84]. Dusek claimed that as technology develops, it forms society and its institutions at the same time and provoke cultural shifts as well. Causal explanations apply to cultural phenomena: accordingly, every event has a previous event or set of causes. Determinists tend to think that 'there is a lawful regularity of the relation of causes and effects' [41:p85], and these in some cases involve predictability as well. Giving causal explanations retrospectively though are always risky, especially technology wise. It is highly difficult to make an argumentation based on speculation like what if we would not have invented cell phones or the internet, thus imagine a path that has not been taken by humankind. Not only because this did not happen, but there is no way to verify a theory like this. Technological determinism as such does receive a lot of criticism partly because of this. Andrew Feenberg, the American philosopher, suggested that technology does not have a single, fixed track, and it is continually adapting to the changing social conditions and demands [48:p113].

Usually, these kinds of arguments are applied in the field of social theory, technological discourses, and philosophy, to name but a few, but they have not been discussed profoundly regarding visual culture and in art history. For this issue that artist for some reason painted better images regarding verisimilitude, traditional art history explains from within the discipline, so from an internal account. It interprets everything within art history and does not emphasize the role of technological progress and specific devices. But, the fact that they addressed technological devices as leading forces in social and art historical context rather than showing them as secondary causes is a determinist viewpoint. They did not include any reference to the philosophy of technology but addressed the topic as a merely art historical one. In my paper what I argue is that this connects at least as much to the philosophy of technology as to art history. Don Ihde's response to the thesis was not that Hockney was wrong, but that he did not discover anything new, only publicized a common knowledge. "What may have been forgotten by some art critics and historians is that how fully technologized the Renaissance and Early Modernity was. Might Galileo without his telescope be analogous to Caravaggio without his camera?" [97, p. 384-85] And he claimed that different types of cameras were epistemology engines, which were models for the production of knowledge.

11.3 Anomalies and the problem of verisimilitude

These assumptions and the Hockney Falco thesis indicate a technological lock-in situation because artists who had a device were indeed in a better position than those who did not, and because art was craftsmanship back then, it is apparent why they were secretive about their working methods. Technological lock-in appears when an artifact becomes a crucial part of a process or artistic attitude: "central to the idea of lock-in is that technologies and technological systems follow paths that are difficult and costly to escape. Consequently, they tend to persist for extended periods, even in the face of competition from potentially superior substitutes [152:p1]." For the better option artist had to wait for hundreds of years, precisely until photography was invented, but this intersection of technology, art, and instrumentation shows that painting in the progress of realism and verisimilitude owes a lot to particular devices. Even though the concept of verisimilitude as such is the baseline of the Hockney-Falco argument, the authors did not give a clear clarification on it but used it as a commonsense term. With this, the line of reasoning is easier to follow, but at the same time, this also means that the sensitive and complex nature of verisimilitude had been ignored.

Verisimilitude as a concept in art refers to a particular property of an art piece: of its resemblance to reality. This as a notion appeared in its earliest form in Plato's philosophy, where he questioned the purpose of art. But verisimilitude has always been highly spatiotemporal and related to other artistic circumstances, and the values attached to it are ever changing. Some representational theories question if this type of faithfulness to reality has any actual artistic value whatsoever [187:p16]. Ernst Gombrich, the famous art historian, claimed that artists are not even capable of copying what they see even if they wanted to. According to him, experimentation 'can show the artist a way out of the prison of style toward a greater truth. Only through trying out new effects never seen before in paint could he learn about nature [60:p320]'. The lenses and mirrors that artists started to use were experiments to make better images regarding representation. These endeavors were pointless nonetheless, claimed a couple of years after Gombrich by Nelson Goodman, mainly because objects and the world around us cannot be copied. He argued that there is no such a thing as *The World*, rather, there are as many worlds as it can be described by people [62:p6]. The problem is that then there are too many opinions, thoughts, and viewpoints of a single object, and it is impossible to represent it in its fullness. The artist must choose an aspect, an angle, but not a random one, rather an ordinary setting. 'The way the object looks to the normal eye, at proper range, from a favorable angle, in good light, without instrumentation, unprejudiced by affections or animosities or interests, and unembellished by thought or interpretation [62:p7]'. Beside many problems, the trickiest part is the instrumentation, considering my main argument. As artists discovered the devices as early as the beginning of the Renaissance, the art historical canon and the notion of verisimilitude became inseparable from technology.

11.4 Summary

Special lenses and mirrors not only helped painters to create such masterpieces but at the same time deformed the paintings in a way that was not obvious at first sight. These changes can be spotted if one looks at small details, like textiles or different patterns on a picture, rather than at the whole painting. The thesis of technological determinism, precisely that technology generates changes and leads society appears when the visual modifications caused by a particular technological device become part of the art historical canon. This not only means the progress regarding realism and perspective but refers to specific mistakes created by these tools as well. If an artist uses a *camera lucida* for example, when the focus moves from the background to the foreground, from one point to another, or if the artist has to move the device or the light moves, the scale and perspectives change, and this result in an image where several different perspectives compose one picture. Placed together the pieces just do not match.

Thus, alongside the progress, anomalies appeared too, and art history has not yet been able to explain them. An internal critic, from a traditional art history point of view, does not give a gratifying account because it does not emphasize the role of technology. Instead, an external determinist view could provide improved answers and a more complex picture of art history. The aim of my ongoing research is, on the one hand, to examine how these modifications became part of traditional art historical canon, and on the other hand, why these mistakes kept appearing even after artist stopped using the tool itself? Artists around the 16th century, for instance, Brueghel, Bosch, or Grünewald did not use optical devices, but were familiar with them, and also it is more than likely that they all seen paintings in which other artists used technological devices. On their pictures, there are effects, like tones, shadows, etc. which were heavily influenced by lenses and other devices even though they did not use them. Hockney and Falco have not talked about how long artists used *camera lucida* or *obscura*, but it is more than likely they kept using it until a better option, photography came and transformed art. Thus, these devices were determinative of the visual canon, and illuminate a reading of art history dominated by technological devices.

Chapter 12

Nudging for Hyperreality: A Philosophical Study of Technological Choice Architectures

Balázs Horváth

Budapest University of Technology and Economics

Summary

This study aims to revisit the ideas of German-born American philosopher of technology, Albert Borgmann about new realities created by technology and machinery in light of how specific technological choice architectures can nudge the human agents into entering a 'hyperreal' environment. The paper introduces a thought experiment which argues that such an environment reduces the agent's choice set to a binary system and that cognitive biases and heuristics provide entry points into this so-called 'technological hyperreality'.

12.1 Motivation

Although Albert Borgmann has not published new works since the release of *Real American Ethics* [19], the work of the German-born American professor in previous decades on philosophy of technology has left a profound impact on the field. Borgmann made his first significant contribution by introducing the notion of the *device paradigm* in his book *Technology and the Character of Contemporary Life* [16]. In 1992, he took on the concepts of *reality* and *postmodernism* in *Crossing the Postmodern Divide* [17]. Various technological advancements and the information revolution in the 21st century have shown Borgmann's concerns about reality and postmodern realism from the 90s valid. Meanwhile a research programme started by Nobel Laureate researcher Daniel Kahneman has continued to grow and has interesting connections to Borgmann's work. The main motivation of this paper is to revisit and reexamine Borgmann's concept of 'hyperreality' with the aim to find the entry point for an individual experience of 'hyperreality' with the help of Kahneman's research programme on heuristics and biases in human decision-making.

12.2 Opting for No Control

My main philosophical argument is shown through the following thought experiment entitled '*Opting for No Control*'.

Let us suppose that driverless (also-known-as self-driving) car technology is sophisticated enough for legal ramifications to be in place allowing the everyday use of such technology on the streets. There is also the presupposition that this legal environment fostered the spread of cars with driverless functions which are now commonplace and in everyday use. However, in the setting of the thought experiment, using the self-driving capability of the cars is not mandatory at all, rather it is a comfort feature like heated seats which can be turned on and off based on the desire of the human driver.

Sue owns such a car, and on a Monday morning she enters it for her daily commute from home to work. Let us examine the choice set of Sue for this trip between points A (her home) and B (her workplace) prior and after acquiring the self-driving enabled vehicle. Before the emergence of driverless cars, Sue had to drive to work herself with her 'regular' car, and since her commute took her through the downtown of the city, she had a huge variety of viable routes from which she preferred three. Her actual decision on a given day depended on the weather, traffic and how late she was for her first meeting. After Sue purchased her new vehicle capable of driving itself, seemingly her choice-set widened: she still had access to her three favourite routes when she felt like driving her car herself, or as an extra option, she could just turn on the 'autopilot' and lean back for the ride. The following points can be made regarding this situation which together can be used to construct the argumentation of the paper.

First, I will show that when Sue turns on the self-driving feature of the car, the state she enters can be described by what Albert Borgmann calls a 'hyperreal' environment or 'hyperreal' experience. I will present a thesis that the widening of the choice set is misleading, and entering hyperreality reduces the choices of the human agent to a binary system: she can either stay in or leave the hyperreal environment.

Secondly, I will argue that Sue makes her decision in a so-called technological choice architecture where she is a subject of the act of manipulation through the use of cognitive biases and heuristics.

12.3 Hyperreality behind the wheel

Borgmann identifies three main characteristic features of his 'hyperreal' environment: a Borgmannian hyperreality is *brilliant, rich* and *pliable* [17:p87-88]. Let us see what these indicators entail in detail, and whether Sue's worriless journey to work in a self-driving car satisfies these prerequisites for hyperreality. Borgmann writes the following in *Crossing the Postmodern Divide*: "*Brilliance has an inclusive and exclusive aspect. It is to include all my senses entirely Technically, brilliance means absence of noise.*" [17:p87] In the thought experiment, I argue that Sue is in such a noiseless, carefree situation; since when she pushes the button for the autopilot, the sensors and the machinery of the car take away every operation. This means that the machine cancels out every outside noise that would normally come with the human operation of a vehicle. Sue can lean back and enjoy the ride without any further external input; her mind is free to wander off during the trip, for daydreaming, for a nap, or for consuming news and other media. By richness, Borgmann means some kind of "*ideal encyclopedic completeness*" [17:p88] as in an extremely lifelike simulation. As the self-driving car is the perfect simulation of a human driver, even more so since the machine can have better sensors and quicker decision-making processes counted in nanoseconds instead of human reaction-time, one can easily identify the experience in a driverless car as a "rich" one. "*Finally, hyperreality is pliable, entirely subject to my desire and manipulation. Technically, pliability includes interactivity*" writes the American philosopher of technology [17:p88]. The driverless vehicle in which Sue travels has indeed such an interactive feature, as Sue (the user) has vast points where she can interact with the AI-powered software that will take her to work, as it is usual nowadays regarding the user experience aspect of software development.

Borgmann uses a collective term for his three features of hyperreality which plays a pivotal role in his later reasoning regarding commodification: *glamour*. To better grasp this term, let us take a look at Borgmann's own examples for hyperreality, which include a visit to Disneyland, or the 'Montana running experience'. The latter is a thought experiment by Borgmann where a Montana resident gets a lucrative employment offer elsewhere in the U.S. However, she loves her daily running exercises in the Montana mountains very much, so her job offer includes paid membership for a gym where she is surrounded by video screens showing her home state on a treadmill video screen, perfectly imitating the 'Montana running experience'. As Borgmann writes: "*The telos of hyperreal logic would be a perfectly glamorous simulator*" [17:p88].

These examples suggest that *glamour* is a somewhat vague yet fitting term. It seems that this common feature of hyperreality can be described as a promise of effortlessness, where we don't have to display any skills or pay any attention, where we are not faced with the hardships of the real world. Another important notion is the discontinuity of hyperreality. As Borgmann writes: *"Disposability and discontinuity are marks of hyperreal glamour, and glamour, in turn is the perfect sign of commodity."* [17:p96]. These two notions have the following consequence. In a hyperreal environment, the human agent has only a binary choice set: she could either stay in this glamorous setting or discontinue the hyperreal experience and return to reality. So the apparent extra choice of Sue should be rather considered as some kind of 'trap' that comes with the radical reduction of the choice set.

The effortlessness of the self-driving option in the car - where the act of transport becomes a commodity - shows the system's own *glamour* before Sue who is 'opting for no control'. Very much like video games have *glamour* for teenage boys, a new iPhone has glamour for Apple fans and Disneyland has glamour for little children. The brilliance, richness and pliableness for the experience of Sue I have noted above. Let us now turn to a question to which Borgmann does not seem to pay enough attention: if hyperreality is indeed disposable and discontinuous, and *"we must sooner or later step out if it into the real world"* [17:p96], then how and why do we enter it in the first place? Is the mere fact that technology surrounds us everywhere a sufficient premise for entering hyperreality, or can the situation be described in a more nuanced way? Looking into these questions, the next part will analyse the so-called 'choice architecture' of Sue before she 'opts for no control'.

12.4 Nudging for hyperreality

The term 'choice architecture' was coined by psychologist of judgement and decision-making Daniel Kahneman and behavioural economist Richard H. Thaler. They wrote the following: *"Decision makers do not make choices in a vacuum. They make them in an environment where many features, noticed and unnoticed, can influence their decisions."* [214]. This can be easily connected with *Churchill's principle* quoted by Borgmann in his book *Real American Ethics*: *"We shape our buildings, and afterwards our buildings shape us."* [19:p5]. The analogy serves as the main motivation when we turn to cognitive biases and heuristics for trying to determine the basis of Sue's decision to initiate the self-driving feature of her car, which as has been argued beforehand is a way for her to enter a hyperreal state.

The research programme for cognitive biases and heuristics was set in motion in the 1970s by the experimental demonstration of three heuristics: availability, representativeness, and adjustment and anchoring [218]. Since then, the programme has spanned numerous results from evolutionary psychology to behavioural economics, including two Nobel Memorial Prizes in Economic Sciences (in 2002, Kahneman received the prize "for having integrated insights from psychological research into economic science, especially concerning human judgment and decision-making under uncertainty", and Thaler followed recently in 2017 "for his contributions to behavioural economics").

The findings of this research area have also gained widespread popularity with the 2006 publication of the New York Times bestseller book "Nudge" [215]. The main idea presented in the book is that humans as a species have underlying cognitive processes (the aforementioned biases and heuristics) that can be utilised with the aim to guide (to 'nudge') people for better judgment in situations where their underlying preferences don't align with their primary preferences, while it can be shown that their underlying preference is the rational choice for them. A classic example of this situation is of a smoking person: her primary preference is getting a cigarette with a coffee after lunch. However, her underlying preference is to quit smoking since she knows it is irrational to keep up with this proven unhealthy habit. Another classic example for a nudge is the visual targets on the inner walls of urinals (e.g. a fly) in public restrooms for gentlemen which are supposed to reduce spillage.

The aforementioned philosophical framing for nudging is called "*libertarian paternalism*", where nudging someone - while looking out for their best interest - is not manipulative, but it tries to preserve the freedom of choice of the nudged person. This could be put into a formal definition in the following way:

> "*Nudge: A nudges B when A makes it more likely that B will ϕ, primarily by triggering B's shallow cognitive processes, while A's influence preserves B's choice-set and is substantially noncontrolling (i.e. preserves B's freedom of choice).*" [190]

Since its original creators did not provide an exact definition for nudging like the one above, and the topic has been as controversial as popular after its inception, this study will solely focus on the biases themselves, which have been proven to exist and to work in choice architectures [78], especially on the so-called status quo bias which states that human agents have a cognitive preference for the current state of things (like when people tend to sit in the same place in a conference from one day to another).

When Sue enters her car and has to choose between driving her vehicle herself on one of her three favourite routes or initiating the self-driving function, she is in a choice architecture which is interwoven with technology and commodification in the terms of Borgmann. As people in the Information Age we are surrounded by so much technology that most of the time the technology itself is the presenter and constructor of our choice sets (i.e. when searching for information online, Google arranges the hits). This is what I have called a 'technological choice architecture'. In the case of Sue, she is applicable to the status-quo bias because the self-driving technology is widespread and widely accepted, as described at the start of the thought experiment. Especially if the software in her car is designed with the driverless feature as the default option, the software could easily present Sue with such a framed question that will serve as an incentive for her to go with the default and enter the 'hyperreal' journey.

As such, in the technological choice architecture, it was a cognitive bias and intentional design choices by the software architects that influenced Sue to step into the hyperreal experience of the driverless journey. In more general terms, the consumerist and commodified digital culture of the present that Borgmann condemns is a ripe playground for the designers and architects of technological innovations. They can easily utilise the shallow cognitive processes of human agents so one will opt for the effortless 'hyperreal' experience. To sum it up, the design of technological choice architectures is laden with the toolset of nudging, which in the end serves as a significant beacon into Borgmann's hyperreality.

12.5 Discussion

In the works of Albert Borgmann, the question of 'hyperreality' is deeply connected with ethical and moral questions - hence the suggestive title of the last published book of Borgmann - as shown in the following quote: "*we must think of experience not as the sum total of sensory stimulation over certain time but as an eminent encounter of a person with the world. A hyperreal setting fails to provide the tasks and blessings that call forth patience and vigor in people.*" [17:p95-96].

However, this short philosophical study was not intended to address the ethical and moral issues, because the texts of Borgmann are value-laden enough with a clear moral compass and suggested 'focal practises' that should help us in "*holding on to reality*" (another book by Borgmann). Instead, the paper addressed some consequences and questions of entering hyperreality: I have presented an original thought experiment which has helped to argue that

1. because of the discontinuous and glamorous nature of hyperreality, such an experience reduces the choice set of the human agent to a binary one (stay or leave);

2. technological choice architectures that enable the utilisation of shallow human cognitive processes called biases and heuristics can provide an entrance into technological hyperreality.

The presented thought experiment, 'Opting for No Control' and the whole hyperreal experience could also be addressed through another psychological research programme instead of biases and heuristics: namely the *flow theory* of Mihály Csíkszentmihályi. The renowned professor of psychology also distinguishes practises based on the effort needed for them and the quality of the activity and states that effortless consumption of virtual media only imitates the real flow experience. This rhymes with Borgmann, whose notion of hyperreality also entails some kind of effortlessness.

There is another aspect regarding hyperreality that is ripe for further research: I am referring to the relationship between video games and modern board games or tabletop games. While the former 'classic' games are clear examples by Borgmann for a hyperreal setting, the latter ones are quite the opposite and represent one of the most important concepts of Borgmann that help us experience reality: the so-called culture of the table. Because for Borgmann, the table is where the family comes together and shares meals and stories, having the aforementioned 'eminent encounters' with each other.

This paper has been concerned with hyperreality in such a way that hopefully convinces the reader of the relevance of Albert Borgmann's ideas to the present day without having to accept the normative stances of the philosopher.

Chapter 13

Technology-based Critical Phenomena: a Borgmannian Approach of Crisis Prediction[1]

Péter Neuman and Dániel Gergő Pintér

Budapest University of Technology and Economics

Summary

Technological development, in general, is intimately related to the different individual and organizational crises that occur in societies. In our paper, we propose a framework for the study of technology-related crises that draws upon the Albert Borgmann introduced term "device paradigm" to help our understanding of human's disengagement from their tools, and ultimately from their environment. We claim that, in a series of cases, ignorance or insufficient knowledge of Borgmann's device paradigm finally led to a crisis-like situation. It is worth noting that the prevention and long-term solutions of those crises have inevitably required the full adoption and understanding of the device paradigm and the development of focal things and practices as a way to mitigate the harmful effect of using postmodern communication technologies and to overcome human reliance upon them. The existence of the device paradigm is not par excellence harmful, instead, it must motivate a new way of looking at the technological environment. In other words, it sets a lower limit of the astuteness people should gain about the technological things, tools that surround them. Crises typical of the Information Age are in some sense similar; however, a new source of crises could occur simply due to the different types of information and information collection ubiquitous to-

---

[1] The research leading to these results was supported by OTKA/NKFIH grant No. K-109456 "Integrated reasoning".

day. Following Borgmann, we observe that information communicated via technology becomes a kind of rival of reality. The distant character of technological information, to use Borgmann's term, can also be viewed as a source of new types of crisis. In this paper, we argue crises may stem from the new character of technological information. By applying Borgmann's characteristics of technological information, we identify other properties of the triggers of that new type of crisis that may serve not only as explanations of the occurrence of real crises but also as indicators of future crisis-like events that are likely to happen. We present a more or less documented case study – Hillary Clinton's email scandal – to show how technology-triggered crises emerge.

13.1 Introduction: unpredictable events as a result of technological development

The present study has a double role, and a twofold target group, correspondingly. Crisis management professionals, and philosophers of technology. For the first group, we are proposing a new tool that can predict, thus avoid crises. The attention of the philosophers of technology we would like to draw to a case, where Borgmann's thoughts about modern technology, the device paradigm are given practical relevance. [16]

The question whether the effects of technological development on mankind are limited to helping the achievement of some predetermined goals has been present in a wide range of disciplines (philosophy of science, philosophy of technology, history of technology, etc.) in the past centuries. It was these goals that initiated the processes, which led to the series of developments of the given form of technology, its existence's *causa efficiens*. The emergence of trains or automobiles made transport much faster, thus contributed to the accessibility of formerly un-accessible places in the short run, and before long these new forms and means of transportation managed to turn the whole world upside down. They changed not only the speed of transportation and activities connected with transportation, but also the new ways of travel had an impact on interpersonal relationships, families, military activities, wars, literature and other forms of art, practically all aspects of human life. The fact that technological changes may have unforeseen effects, therefore, is by no means a new phenomenon. [16]

Thus, it is no surprise that the naive "means to an end" approach to technology is replaced by looking at technology as a certain kind of human activity. Nevertheless, the teleological nature of technological development cannot and should not be neglected. We could argue here that technological development nowadays is a costly exercise, that requires either contributions from generous donors (like states) and/or promising business plans. No finance is possible without reasonably formulated predetermined goals, in other words, we need to have intelligent predictions about the future use of the technological device we are working on, and these predictions have to be acceptable to the relevant stakeholders. But this is only one, and possibly not the most important aspect of the teleological nature of technological development. It does not seem to be possible to invent the steam engine, for example, if we have no idea what we want to do with it.

Hence, technological development may have certain malicious side effects. Side effects, we can usually predict. However, there are cases when it is impossible to see in advance the unfavourable and unwanted results of technological development. There are several models of technological development, some of them are even non-linear[2], generating chaos. Without going into the details of the chaotic behaviour of technological development, we can say that the impact of it can be unpredictable and malicious. The unforeseeability in a naïve approach can be the result of two disjoint factors:

1. The peculiar (chaotic) dynamics of the system. In this case we know everything about the technology (all the boundary conditions, using physics terms), but the laws that govern the development introduce non-linearity into the system, which will result in chaotic, unpredictable behaviour.

2. The unpredictable behaviour is the result of the lack of knowledge of the interaction between technology and humans.

Both factors may contribute to the emergence of unpredictable impact. Unpredictability plays a special role in crises. The fact that we are not able to see beforehand how a crisis develops, what fields it enters is one of the factors that distinguishes the chaotic regime from a normal series of events. Although, unpredictability is an inevitable constituent of crises, predicting the emergence of critical situations is not always impossible. Early signs of crisis emergence can be identified. In fact, this is what we are aiming at in this paper. The purpose of the present study is to contribute to the understanding of crisis emergence as a result of technological development. Using the technology philosophical thoughts of Albert Borgmann, mainly his concept about the device paradigm, we propose a method that can help to predict the emergence of technology-caused crises. The crisis management professional needs to be able to predict crises in her everyday practice.

---

[2] See e.g. [90]

Crisis prevention, in general, includes methods that are intended to keep people or organizations from experiencing a future individual or institutional crisis. They include teaching strategies and counselling to increase stabilization. For crises, these often focused on early identification of situations that stimulate crisis or indications of destabilization. Crisis intervention refers to strategies and responses used once signs of crisis are already present. They can reduce the impact of the crisis immediately. They can also ameliorate long-term problems. [181]

13.2 Crisis Management and Communication Technology in the Information Society

We know that the development of communication technology and the change of media consumption habits have changed the environment in such a way that event series that did not generate a crisis decades ago result in the clear development of critical situations today. [157] New information platforms show up every other day, which can result in the emergence of uncontrolled streams of information. The situation is made even more complicated because many people are not able to use these platforms/channels properly.

On the other hand, the development of communication technology introduced brand new tools that can be used for crisis management. [157] After 2010 corporate executives started to include the Internet into their crisis management toolbox. [153] Budgets to be used for online communication grew. Companies allocate resources to developing crisis management taking place in social media. We may say that the internet-based technologies not only changed the logic and the protocol of crisis management, but they also helped us to constantly monitor the scene of potential problems, prepare for the emergence of crises, and also facilitate quick and effective crisis responses. [61]

The appearance of the *information society* has totally rearranged the access to information [6]. Information technology imposes pressure on society for getting stimulation and news consumption never experienced before. [159:p676] The structure of the world has become network-based, where internet and online communication stepped forward as a faith defining experience. [27] Being network based is just one of the characteristics of the information society that contributes to so far unknown triggers of malevolent peculiar series of events. As we shall see, the information society and the new technology have other means too for crisis genesis.

Before going into details, in order to avoid confusion about the meaning of the term crisis, let us summarize what is generally meant by this phenomenon. The word "crisis" comes from the Greek word κρίσις /"krizei" whose meaning is decision, resolution or turn. With English intermediation, the concept can be defined as a critical state, hardship or a hazardous situation occurring in the life of a person or a group, and as such is accompanied by operational problems and conflicts. [21:p2] The word is often used as synonym of "distress", since both are a process of feeling tense, threatened, hopeless and lost [31:p19], which is not only significantly loading the troubleshooting capacity of the involved ones, but also bears the possibility of turning to negative or positive direction. [213:p2]

Crisis has several defining characteristics. Seeger, Sellnow, and Ulmer say that crises have four defining characteristics that are:

> "specific, unexpected, and non-routine events or series of events that create high levels of uncertainty and threat or perceived threat to an organization's high priority goals." [196:p233]

Based on this approach Venette argues that "crisis is a process of transformation where the old system can no longer be maintained." [220:p43]

Therefore the fourth defining quality is the need for change. If change is not needed, the event could more accurately be described as a failure.

The most significant professions dealing with the features of different crises, like management, communication and psychology identified four primary characteristics of the concept. [21] analysed international management journals publishing studies about crises. Despite the diversity of the different scientific perspectives and the multiplicity of intellectual traditions, the following general features were attributed to crises:

- crises induce uncertainty and disturbances and request a change of former management or communication practice [102]

- crises endangering the image, reputation and public relations of the organisations [158, 97],

- as a definitive part of a longer complex process, crises attract great public interest [98, 184],

- crises are in close relation with individual or group behaviour, accordingly, they can be considered as socially constructed phenomena bearing several subjective interpretations [30:p478].

The profession and the scientific community interpret crises as events outstanding from the everyday routine, occurring mainly unforeseen and potentially endangering the implementation of the objectives. [196:p233] The demolishing phenomena at the same time also brings the recognition that the former processes are not sustainable under the current circumstances [220:p43]. Thus the zero point of successful management of a hazardous situation is actually "a decision made with the aim of reaching a turn accompanied by setting up alterations, their management and communication" [156:p36].

Apart from natural crises that are inherently unpredictable (volcanic eruptions, tsunami etc.) most of the crises that we face are created by man. Hence the requirements of their being 'unexpected' depends upon man failing to note the onset of crisis conditions. Some of our inability to recognise crises before they become dangerous is due to the lack of understanding what is going on. During the crisis management process, it is important to identify types of crises in that different crises necessitate the use of different crisis management strategies [29]. Potential crises are enormous, but crises can be clustered. [108] categorized eight types of crises:

- Natural disaster
- Technological crises
- Confrontation
- Malevolence
- Organizational Misdeeds
- Workplace Violence
- Rumours
- Terrorist attacks/man-made disasters

Technological crises are caused by humans using science and technology. Technological accidents inevitably occur when technology becomes complex and coupled and something goes wrong in the system as a whole (technological breakdowns). Some technological crises occur when human error causes disruptions (human breakdowns). People tend to assign blame for a technological disaster because technology is subject to human manipulation whereas they do not hold anyone responsible for a natural disaster. When an accident creates significant environmental damage, the crisis is categorized as megadamage. Examples include software failures, industrial accidents, and oil spills [29, 103].

13.3 The Device Paradigm: a Bormannian approach to understanding the nature of postmodern technology

We saw that crises are intimately related to the development of technology. The very existence of modern devices can cause critical behaviour, and modern technological tools in communication and elsewhere have an impact on how critical situations should and can be managed. [157] We would like to distinguish a special type of crisis from other technology-driven phenomena. The crisis we have in mind emerges because of insufficient and inadequate knowledge of technology. We can call this type of crises postmodern. It is important to see that it is not only that the users do not know how to use the new piece of technology. They do not even understand and do not even realize what may be going on. And this prevents them from:

- identifying the critical situation,

- finding the right answers, measures and solutions to handle the crisis,

- drawing the right conclusions in order to prevent a future crisis.

We shall see an example of this very type of crises in the next section. The nature of these types of crises can be captured with the help of Borgmann's device paradigm concept. The device paradigm includes the effects of the introduction of the technological devices, the impact of the emergence of the "thing", that helps us reach a certain goal, the thing that has been thought of originally as a means to an end and nothing else. [18]

According to Borgmann, the availability of the technological device is the necessary condition of its existence as technological device. The availability, in this case, includes the fulfilment of four conditions, namely the commodity needs to be instantaneous, ubiquitous, safe and easy. [18] There is absolutely no doubt that digital technology fulfils all four conditions. Moreover, we may say that the fact that digitalization is present in all aspects of our modern life, is strongly connected to its meeting Borgmann's conditions. Borgmann writes:

> "division between the commodity, e.g., music, and the machinery, e.g., the mechanical and electronic apparatus of a stereo set, that is the distinctive feature of a technological device" [18:p217].

Thus the distance between the machinery of the technological device and us plays a crucial role here. While heating the room by starting a fireplace fire is a high level of technological development, in one sense it is quite different from how information technology works. In the introductory chapter of his book about Information technology, Borgmann summarizes one key feature of IT as follows:

> "In addition to the information that discloses what is distant in space and remote in time, there is information that allows us to trans- form reality and make it richer materially and morally" [18:p1].

Borgmann actually defines the potential problem begging for a solution.

"A thing, in the sense in which I want to use the word here, is inseparable from its context, namely, its world, and from our commerce with the thing and its world, namely, engagement. The experience of a thing is always and also a bodily and social engagement with the thing's world. In calling forth a manifold engagement, a thing necessarily provides more than one commodity. The technological information on a compact disc is so detailed and controlled that it addresses us virtually as reality. What comes from a recording of a Bach cantata on a CD is not a report about the cantata nor a recipe-the score-for performing the cantata, it is in the common understanding music itself. Information through the power of technology steps forward as a rival of reality. Today the three kinds of information are layered over" [17:p41].

We may say that it is the crisis that abolishes the tension generated by the disengagement of humans from the device.[3] Here we are in a position to formulate our first thesis. At this stage, we outline it as a possibility of disengagement, but in the next section, we will show a real example endorsing it.

The disengagement between user and machinery of a given device can generate stubborn crises, that the stakeholders are not able to identify, prevent and handle.

---

[3] Almost a century before Borgmann Max Weber referring to science and technology wrote about the concept of disenchantment. Disenchantment can also be viewed as a result of technological and scientific development. Both disenchantment and disengagement are referred to as negative phenomena, however, there is a core difference between the two. While disenchantment is the product of humans starting to think differently about religion, mysticism, thus this is an absolutely conscious process, a result of cognitive processes. Disengagement on the other hand is something we are unaware about, and it is this feature that makes it dangerous according to Borgmann. [223]

13.4 A postmodern crisis: the Clinton email controversy

In March 2015, it became publicly known that Hillary Clinton, during her tenure as United States Secretary of State, had used her family's private email server for official communications, rather than official State Department email accounts maintained on federal secure servers. Those official communications included over 100 emails which contained classified information at the time they were sent, as well as nearly 2,100 emails which were not marked classified but would retroactively be ranked as classified by the State Department. [141]

The controversy unfolded against the backdrop of Clinton's 2016 presidential election campaign and hearings held by the United States House Select Committee on Benghazi. Some experts and members of Congress have contended that her use of private messaging system software and a private server violated State Department protocols and procedures, as well as federal laws and regulations governing recordkeeping. In response, Clinton has said that her use of personal email was in compliance with federal laws and State Department regulations and that former secretaries of state had also maintained personal email accounts, though not their own private email servers. [147]

The Federal Bureau of Investigation (FBI) initiated an investigation regarding the origin and handling of classified emails on Clinton's server. The FBI found that all classified emails on Clinton's server were stored and sent from "*unclassified systems*", violating the same policies as those on Clinton's personal server. The FBI identified 110 emails as containing information that was classified at the time it was sent, including 65 emails deemed "*Secret*" and 22 deemed "*Top Secret*". An additional three email chains contained "portion markings", simply a "(C)" indicating "*Confidential*" in front of one or more paragraphs. [147]

Clinton told the FBI she did not know the meaning of "(C)".

FBI's investigation had concluded that Clinton was "extremely careless" in handling her email system but recommended that no charges be filed against her. [44] It is needless to say now, that the scandal had an extremely strong impact on the pending presidential election. [147]

The Clinton email scandal shows that **if she understood the concept she would have been more cautious, and if she had not been disengaged from the machinery she would have understood that the situation is critical and may evolve in a completely unpredictable form.**

These findings are endorsed by the following facts: multiple statements by Clinton seem to prove that she simply did not get it.

- "*I never sent or received any classified material.*" [217]

- "*It wasn't the best choice. I made a mistake. It was not prohibited. It was not in any way disallowed.*" [141]

Although as a lawyer Clinton should be aware that:

> "it is a misdemeanor punishable by fines and imprisonment for a federal employee to knowingly remove classified information without authority and with the intent to retain such documents or materials at an unauthorized location."[4]

Based on what we learnt from the Clinton email scandal, we can formulate our second thesis: signs of disengagement can be identified even in the pre-crisis state. These can serve as early indicators of potential crises. The way out from this could be the abolishment of the disengagement. Details of this will be elaborated in a next study.

13.5 Conclusions and further research

Our study is by no means a comprehensive or detailed analysis. We are proposing a way or a method of looking at crises that are related to information technology. We believe that having in mind the lessons learnt from the Clinton email scandal, we can understand more about the causes of certain critical situations that emerge quite often these days.

Following Borgmann, our basic conclusion is the following:

the farther we are from the machinery (in the sense that we do not own, do not master the technology, cannot make changes to it on our own), unforeseen effects become more likely. Such unforeseen effects contribute to the development and emergence of crises in unusual ways.

We have learnt that crisis indicators can change dramatically: It is not surprising that the time it takes for a crisis to develop is of crucial importance, even from a practical point of view. The less time we have for preparation for crisis management, the weaker our response can be. We introduce the term, abbreviation to take care of it, called time to crisis (TTC). It is also apparent that the time needed for crisis (TTC) development can be much shorter, or alternatively: the time scale becomes unusual. Another peculiarity is that there is no such thing as expiry of crisis causing events, in other words, *the internet does not forget*.

---

[4] 18 U.S. Code § 1924, United States Code 2006 Edition pp.429

It is not only the distance understood in a figurative sense, between the machinery and us that comes into the picture but also the distance between the crisis causing event, a major term in crisis handling, (we will abbreviate it by CCE) and the emergence of the crises in time.

- Thesis1: TTC can be much shorter than before.

- Thesis2: CCE never expires.

- Thesis3: Device crises may not be avoided, however, the possibility of their emergence may be predictable.

Thus,

- we can prepare for them,

- models can be created and studied; what we have in mind here is to look at real case studies just like fictional ones in order to understand how much the disengagement and the insufficient knowledge of the device paradigm can be implicated with the development. It would be desirable to be able to set up some kind of a gauge or measure to see how efficient the disengagement as a CCE is.

- instead of denial, complete transparency should be considered in the communication.

Our theses are based on the Clinton case study. It actually indicates the validity of the device paradigm concept and its relevance and usefulness in the study of crises. However, comprehensive research can and should be done in order to qualitatively determine the strength of such CCE's. We believe that it can be done, nevertheless, case studies should be looked at in a significant number. The good news is that there is no shortage of such events in the literature and in the press. After looking at case studies, identifying the indicators of the crisis will lay the groundwork for a comprehensive analysis of technology-related crises supported with advice on managing them. As a side effect of the proposed case study analyses, with the introduction of the indicators mentioned above, a taxonomy of the different types of device crises can be developed – belonging to different device types.

Chapter 14

The Problem of Undermined Evidence: Accurate Entitlement for Epistemic Systems in Automatic Decision Support Systems

Ákos Gyarmathy

Budapest University of Technology and Economics

Summary

This paper argues for the claim that decision support systems should utilize what is called Jeffrey conditionalization instead of classic Bayesian conditionalization to determine probabilities of an event. My main argument is that classic Bayesian conditionalization requires any condition, including evidence, to be certain in order to determine the probability of the event or statement for which a certain evidence serves as condition. However, the certainty of evidence is an ideal that is seldom achieved because of various, well-known epistemic reasons. Most of the time evidence seems to be uncertain due to methodological errors and hence calculating with the certainty of evidence most probably leads to inaccurate results in determining the probability of the event in question. Jeffrey conditionalization on the other hand, provides a function to calculate the probabilities of events involving conditional probability and makes it possible to do so with using uncertain evidence. Consequently, such probabilistic reasoning will be more accurate than the classical Bayesian method in cases of uncertain evidence, providing a more realistic approach to handling data.[1]

---

[1] My work has been supported by the MTA BTK "Morals and Science" Lendület Project. 2017-287.

14.1 Introduction

What is a decision support system and why it is interesting? Even without establishing an accurate definition, it seems to be safe to say, that decision support systems are automatized systems to support decision making (which are particularly popular in the fields of medical science). Such systems might not involve any computers, and while, the present paper is mainly concerned with computerized decision support systems the general philosophical challenge can be easily extended to automatized or formal decision making in general (Cf. [175])

This paper aims to offer an analysis and a possible improvement of the reasoning systems underlying decision support systems. After the introduction explains why the problem of decision support systems is an interesting philosophical problem, the first two sections focus on defining decision support systems in order to show, that they all share the same reasoning system. First I provide a short historical introduction to the concept of decision support systems then, I attempt to set up a consensual baseline definition for the concept that is agreed upon in the literature. The third section provides a general account of the reasoning structure within decision support systems with the aim of showing their limitations by emphasizing the limitations of classic Bayesian conditionalization. The fourth section introduces Jeffrey conditionalization as a viable candidate for interpreting conditional probability by the reasoning subsystems in decision support systems showing its epistemic advances compared to classic Bayesian conditionalization. This section also provides arguments for improving the reasoning structure within these systems and argues that automatic decision making can be more accurate if these systems abandon the concept of classic Bayesian conditional probability.

Decision support systems are systems that take over and automatize (even if only partially) one of the most human tasks, decision making. In order to be useful, any decision support system, if it proves to be an effective tool, need to be autonomous to a certain degree and need to take over some tasks from human agents. Comparing them to simple calculators reveals their unique role. A simple calculator processes information by using simple functions taking over the task of these calculations from human agents. In order to be a useful tool, the calculators need to perform these tasks without the supervision of the human agent. A decision support system works in a similar way as it takes over the task of ranking different possible solutions for the problem presented by the human agent. The system's (partial) autonomy is provided by its service of taking over cognitive tasks from human agents, however it is not always trivial that these tasks can be formalized. For example, forming an expert opinion on the problem of determining the possible disease responsible for a certain group of symptoms often requires medical expertise which is usually evaluated on the successfulness of the expert in question (i.e. reliability). Since we do not entirely understand successful expertise, it is difficult to formalize such processes which leave the user with two options, concerning the autonomy of such systems. It is either that a human supervisor will always be necessary for such systems, which requires the human agent to solve the problem too in order to supervise the decision made by the system, or to give full autonomy to the system in solving the problem at issue. The first solution makes decision support system to be less effective since the cognitive capacity freed up by the system will remain limited. The second solution, on the other hand, requires the formal reproduction of expert decision making for the domain the system is implemented for.

In reality, the level of autonomy of decision support systems is located between the two extremes. These systems work with a constant but limited expert supervision which provides them with a certain level of autonomy. For such systems to be effective, it will always be a requirement to take over a certain task of complex decision making from human agents. This situation poses the interesting philosophical question: whether effective decision making can be (at least partially) formalized or is it something that only human agents are capable of.

While this paper does not aim to answer the general question of whether decision making can be (at least partially) formalized as a process, its argumentation remains relevant to that question. Since scholars can only answer this question by looking at current implementations of decision support systems, it is vital to understand how these systems work. It is also crucial in answering the general question whether the actually implemented systems are successful enough. However, if the wrong foundations of decision support systems make them inevitably fail then our basis for answering the question of whether decision making can be formalized will be substantially erroneous. My claim is that in their present form, decision support systems are highly limited in interpreting the data available for processing because their reasoning system is not sophisticated enough to properly handle the uncertainty of evidence. This paper offers a more sophisticated function to deal with uncertainties that can eliminate a great deal of the current limitations of these systems that make them less accurate than human agents. Other improvements might also be necessary for replicating expert decision making, but reflecting on these would obviously exceed the ambitions of this paper.

14.2 What is a decision support system? The brief history of the concept

Concerning the importance and the role of decision support systems, [23] describe their role as crucial for processing information on a scale that is available these days:

> "After all, survival and success in this increasingly turbulent, complicated, interdependent world demands astute decision making which, in turn, benefits from the DSS ability to relax cognitive, temporal, and economic limits of decision makers – amplifying decision makers' capacities for processing knowledge which is the lifeblood of decision making." [23:px]

The novelty of this situation seems to have crucial philosophical importance. Decision support systems automatize certain procedures in the working environment that have been the exclusive territory for human agents (mostly experts) in the preceding time. Witnessing the growth of information available for processing by decision makers, decision support systems seem to be an indispensable tool for decision making. However, the expression "decision support system" still lacks a rigorous definition for decades until the 1980s.

[43] provides an extensive genealogy of the term "decision support system" pointing out that the term begins its official career around 1974:

> However, decision support systems (DSS) have already existed long before the term has been created. These or similar systems had been labelled by the names of computer-aided decision systems [53], computer-based decision systems [194], computer-based management decision systems [209], decision calculus [110], decision and information systems [104], decision-information systems [130], decision-oriented information systems [11], information and decision systems [16], management information decision systems [37], man-machine decision systems [56], man-machine planning systems [219], and management support systems [131]. *"In 1994, several authors used the term decision support systems [1, 119]. Although the idea of using computers for making better decisions was published as early as 1963, the idea described by [53] is considered to be the first one discussing the basic idea of DSS in the DSS literature."* [43:p49]

The term 'decision support' first appears in the 1970s (cf. [14, 18]) and rapidly becomes an important field of scholarly research. [14, 18-19] concludes that the various attempts to define decision support in the 1970s agree that:

> *"the system must aid a decision maker in solving unprogrammed, unstructured (or "semistructured") problems(...) the system must possess an interactive query facility, with a query language that resembles English (...). The query facility typically permits ad hoc (...) queries for retrieval (...)."* [14:p18-19]

Besides the common features of decision support systems that make it suitable for human-machine interaction, it is also emphasized that decision support systems do not make autonomous decisions due to their limited capabilities:

> "For instance, the system may have no intrinsic power or authority; it has authority only in proportion to the weight that the decision maker attaches to its activities. For each of the abilities, the machine participates in the joint human-computer decision activity only to the extent that the ability can be formally expressed. For example, the facet of evaluation may involve some nonformalizable subjective processes." [14:p39]

14.3 A consensual definition of decision support systems in the current literature

Recently decision support systems are defined as domain-specific computer-based information systems that integrate data collection, analysis, report and modelling decision making in order to operationalize the process of managerial decision making:

> *"A Decision Support System is a class of highly sophisticated, computer-based information systems employed by executives, managers, or policy makers to serve specific functionalities in managing corporate finance, marketing, planning, and operations..."* [197]

Furthermore, the behaviour of such systems is determined by three major components: the language, the problem processor (the software) and the information about the problem domain, available for the system. The problem processor acquires information from either a human agent or a database.

> *"Commonly, it integrates computer tools for data collection, analysis, and report, with decision models to support the organization's management. Typically, this occurs through gathering information from the organization's business processes and the marketplace to offer relatively abstract knowledge as the basis for timelier and better-considered decisions."* [197]

While the design of the problem processor may be subject to alternatives, [208] explains that decision support systems are generally structured on the same mathematical foundations. This claim can be easily supported by acknowledging the fact that the recent research on decision support systems is mainly focused on information management and human-machine interaction instead of the evaluation of the available options as possible solutions and choosing the best action available (which is the deliberative process itself). Accordingly, the structure of reasoning in these systems is interpreted as their capability for evaluating the information available and ranking possible outcomes, and appears to be based on the same mathematical grounds that were established in the 1970s (cf. [39]).

For instance, according to [208], clinical decision support systems, in general, are grounded on three major mathematical pillars: set theory, Boolean logic and Bayesian probability. Since the focus of this paper is mainly related to the problem of conditional probability in the deliberative models within these systems, I will narrow my reflection on the limitations of the classic Bayesian approach applied in decision support systems.

14.4 Reasoning by decision support systems: the fundamentals of the Bayesian framework

Decision making often invites expressions of uncertainty such as probably, unlikely, certainly, or almost certainly. These expressions indicate chances of events from the range of absolute certainty through different degrees of certainty to the extreme of impossibility (absolute lack of certainty).

Different expression of certainty may refer to events or states of affairs, and accordingly, they are attached to statements referring to them in order to express their probability. For instance, there is a clear intuitive difference between the meaning of the following three statements: 1) "it is impossible that Frederick will be hit by a lightning tomorrow" 2) "it is unlikely that Frederick will be hit by a lightning tomorrow" and that 3) "Frederick will be certainly hit by a lightning tomorrow". While modal expressions such as necessity, impossibility or contingency might sufficiently express the intuitive differences mentioned above, there is a further problem with basic modal terms, namely that not all the contingent events have the same probability or certainty. Since contingency merely means non-necessity and non-impossibility, mere contingency is rather too vague to express the fine-grained differences between different probabilities of events. For example, the following two events both seem to be possible: P: the current president of the United States resigns tomorrow; Q: I will survive typing the next sentence. On the one hand, Q seems to be almost absolutely certain with the exception of unlikely events happening in the next few seconds such as "I will be killed by an assassin" or "I will have a sudden heart attack". On the other hand, P can be considered as a generally unlikely event. While these two are both contingent events, their chances clearly differ and this difference is not expressed by the basic modal term "contingency".

In order to express such differences between the chances of different events, Bayesians offer a gradual scale of chances and assign numerical values to different chances between 0 and 1. They assign 0 probability to impossible events and 1 to necessary events. The rest of the values between the two extremes (0 and 1) are assigned to contingent events, given that the higher the value, the higher the probability of the assigned event, states of affairs or the truth of a statement. This way Bayesians can express the different probabilities of contingent events, states of affairs and the truth of statements[2]. For example, one can assign 0.1 probability to the statement of P: the current president of the United States resigns tomorrow; and 0.99 probability to the statement of Q: I will survive typing the next sentence.

Bayesians also axiomatically determine the relative probabilities of separate events (cf. [101]; cf. [99]; cf. [202]). For instance, intuitively the probability of one event is always higher than the probability of two events happening in conjunction (rule of conjunction). Also, the probability of one event is always lower than the probability of two events in disjunctive relation (rule of disjunction). The only exceptions from the above two rules are the cases where both events belong to the extremes of 1 or 0 probability. One of the most important Bayesian function for decision making is the function of conditional probability. For example, the probability of intelligent life on Mars depends on the probability of life on Mars since intelligent life requires life. With the help of a method called conditionalization, Bayesians can determine the conditional probability of one event, given that a further event (the condition) happens with certainty.

Conditional probability and conditionalization are also important tools for determining the probability of an event or the truth of a statement if it is dependent on any kind of evidence. For example, the probability of my statement that "it will rain tomorrow" being true can be dependent on the weather forecast report. Take the following example. If the probability of "it will rain tomorrow", given that the weather forecast says that "it will rain tomorrow" is 0.8 then you can perform the following inference. If the weather forecast says that "it will rain tomorrow" (so the event of the report happens with probability 1), then you can calculate the probability of rain tomorrow to be 0.8. Conditional probability is a powerful tool in determining probabilities compared to simple prior probabilities. For instance, one might believe that the prior probability of rain (i.e. its probability without any condition involved) tomorrow is 0.5, without any further considerations (it will or will not rain). However, if the weather forecast also predicts rain and if the conditional probability of rain tomorrow is 0.8 given that the weather forecast predicts rain for tomorrow then one can calculate that the probability of rain is higher than the prior

---

[2] According to some interpretations of the Bayesian framework, these values express the objective chances of the events, states of affairs and the statements expressing them but this interpretation is not exclusive and many refuse it.

probability of rain tomorrow if the weather forecast predicts it. Since these rules are merely syntactic rules, they determine relative probability only, therefore the question of the probability of rain without the weather forecast or the question of the conditional probability of rain tomorrow given that the weather forecast predicts it is not answered by using these rules. These rules only determine relative probabilities in the sense as it is determined in the case of conditional probability: if the conditional probability of rain tomorrow, given the weather forecast predicts rain for tomorrow is 0.8 then if the weather forecast predicts rain for tomorrow (probability 1) then the probability of rain tomorrow is 0.8. The problem with this function is that the probability of the condition is always understood as certainty (1) which leads to difficult epistemic and methodological problems.

14.5 The problem of uncertain evidence

Decision support systems use data or (ideally) expert opinion as evidence in order to predict an event or determine its probability and offer suggestions for the best course of action. The structure of reasoning in these systems is dominantly Bayesian which entails that they use conditional probability to calculate the probability of outcomes on the basis of the data available. However, using classical conditionalization would require evidence to be at the level of certainty, but evidence is rarely certain in empirical sciences. Therefore the classical models of conditional probability seem to lead to inaccurate results because of the difference between the probability of the evidence and certainty required for calculating conditional probability.

The problem of evidence

The main role of evidence is to support justified judgements and beliefs that are supported by reason (cf. [176]). Such judgements serve as the basis for predictions and representations of situations during decision making (cf. [224]; cf. [227]). Conditional probability can appear in decision making at least two crucial points. On the representation side, it might determine the agent's representation of the situation of the decision making based on the agent's other beliefs serving as evidence. On the action and planning side, conditional probabilities can serve as the basis of the agent's practical inferences concerning the consequences of the agent's own actions. Both kinds of conditional probabilities involve a certain amount of uncertainty. On the representative side, evidence might be uncertain in the case of a not completely reliable source of evidence. On the action side, the agent might not be certain of the success of her own actions which can undermine the certainty of the utility of a choice or the availability of further options that would have been secured with a successful attempt. For example, an agent might have

The Problem of Undermined Evidence

unreliable evidence to believe that he can make a jump over a gap. In the process of planning, she might see attempting the jump to be a high-risk high benefit option. According to the agent's plan, if the jump is successful, then he can reach a valuable good (e.g. food) and does not need to look for it elsewhere. However, since it is a high-risk choice, the agent needs to consider that this plan might not be realized if her attempt for the jump fails. Apparently, uncertainty plays a crucial role in decision making. For present purposes and because the role of evidence is a more vital issue for decision support systems, it is sufficient to discuss uncertainty for the representative case which is mainly the uncertainty of evidence.

It is widely agreed upon that evidence justifies beliefs. Evidentialists (cf. [28] claim that it is exactly one's total evidence that justifies one's belief. Others (cf. [59]; cf. [177]; cf. [206]; cf. [207]) also acknowledge the role of evidence in justification but deny its exclusivity, because they claim that there are other epistemically relevant cognitive features that also play an important role in justification (e.g. epistemic virtues). But it is still widely agreed upon that evidence plays a crucial role in justification which determines the agent's representation of her situation during deliberation.

The epistemic status of evidence determines the epistemic status of the belief it justifies. For instance, a belief that is supported by an unreliable source would have a similarly weak epistemic status. Therefore to estimate the epistemic status of a judgement, one needs to evaluate the epistemic status of the evidence. In probabilistic terms, the epistemic status of a statement can be expressed in its probability, or the degree of confidence the agent has in the statement in question. If the agent is completely certain about a certain statement, then she will believe that the statement is certainly true therefore its probability is 1. The same is true for the epistemic status of the evidence. The agent is more accurate in her judgements if it is aware of the epistemic status of her judgements and also the epistemic status of her evidence. A decision support system can also provide more accurate results if it also reports the epistemic status of not only the judgements provided by the evidence supporting these judgements. Concerning agents, there is an elaborate epistemic debate discussing the necessity of such reports, called the interalism-externalism debate about justification.

According to internalists, justified belief requires the agent to recognize the epistemic status of her own belief and evidence. Externalist strategy, deny the necessity of such reflexive judgements and claim that justification depends solely on the consequences of the epistemic enterprise that the agent has. If the agent has a belief that is reliable or safe enough then the agent is justified in her belief even if she does not know the epistemic status of her own beliefs. Therefore, according to externalists, the agent is somewhat blind concerning the epistemic status of her own beliefs. According to the internalist strategy, the epistemic status of one's belief mainly depends on the evidence that justifies the belief. Since the agent needs to know the epistemic status of her belief, she also needs to know the epistemic status of her evidence. The problem is that the epistemic status of one's evidence is revealed by the epistemic status of further evidence, therefore in order to know the epistemic status of one's evidence, one needs to know the epistemic status of one's further evidence which quickly leads to an infinite regress of justifying one's evidence.

There are two major strategies to stop the regress of justification: coherentism and foundationalism. Coherentism, on the one hand, requires justified beliefs to be coherent with other beliefs held by the agent, which means to be free from substantial contradictions[3]. Foundationalism, on the other hand, requires one's system of evidence to be traceable to a certain type of evidence which is unquestionable. If one's body of evidence stands on unquestionable evidence, then its epistemic status is considered to be justified without question, for instance, a set of axioms, a set of methodological standards or empirical data.

[205] argues that the above picture is somewhat misleading. Since coherentists argue that the epistemic status of one's beliefs is determined by their coherence with the agent's other beliefs, it is not true that coherentism is a different strategy from foundationalism. Logical consistency between the beliefs provides an unquestionable foundation for this system of belief which is based on a certain interpretation of logic. This interpretation of logic and consistency has the same epistemic status as the foundational beliefs proposed by foundationalists. Hence, Sosa argues that foundationalism and coherentism have the same general structure, which leaves coherentism with the same major worries that foundationalists face.

For foundationalism, the main problem is the question of defining foundational beliefs and justifying their epistemic status. Since they claim that these beliefs do not require epistemic justification, if one's set of beliefs and system of evidence is grounded on them, one can safely state that her justified beliefs are really justified. However, the claim that the epistemic status of certain beliefs, certain axioms or empirical evidence in general, are unquestionable seems to be arbitrary. While identifying foundational beliefs cuts the regress, if it is done arbitrarily, then the epistemic status of one's system of beliefs will depend on one's choice of the foundation and the epistemic status of this foundation.

---

[3] Minor contradictions can be interpreted as insignificant and unavoidable, but for ideal agents it would be also required that one's set of beliefs should be free from any contradictions.

The Problem of Undermined Evidence

So the good thing about internalism is that it requires the agent to know the epistemic status of her own beliefs which entails knowing the epistemic status of her evidence (all of it). The difficulty with this is that it seems to be possible only by an epistemically unquestionable foundation.

A further concern about evidence is its certainty. In epistemology, there are two major approaches to the question of the certainty of evidence: fallibilism and infallibilism. Fallibilists think that a belief can be fallible yet justified which means that even beliefs that are not 100% certain can serve as evidence or constitute knowledge. Infallibilists, on the other hand, think that a belief can only be justified if it is impossible for the belief to be false. Therefore, only certain beliefs can be justified and serve as evidence or constitute knowledge. Infallibilism combined with internalism seems to be inevitably impossible since it would require justified beliefs to be certain. However, there are no epistemically unquestionable foundational beliefs. For decision support systems this is a crucial difficulty because Bayesian conditional probability is defined as the probability of a statement given a piece of evidence is present with certainty. Therefore, in order to determine the probability of an event, based on its conditional probability relative to a certain piece of evidence, the agent needs to know that the evidence is present with certainty. However, such judgements would require infallibilist-internalist approach, which seems to be impossible, due to epistemic considerations.

Fallibilists, on the other hand, can accept that a piece of evidence is not always certain. This aspect of fallibilism is a powerful epistemic tool since it does not only affect the system of evidence one has as a subject of epistemic judgements but also one's reflexive judgements concerning the level of certainty of one's belief. For example, a fallibilist might think that the belief that it will rain tomorrow is based on the weather forecast and the weather forecast is only 50% accurate. Futhermore, a fallibilist can estimate the epistemic status of the evidence that the weather forecast uses and also the epistemic status of the judgement concerning the level of certainty of the weather forecast.

14.6 The solution to the uncertainty problem

As [212] defines it, the simple principle of conditionalization is if we begin with initial or prior probabilities Pi, and we acquire new evidence which can be represented as becoming certain of an evidentiary statement E, "*then rationality requires that one systematically transform one's initial probabilities to generate final or posterior probabilities Pf by conditionalizing on E - that is: Where S is any statement, $Pf(S) = Pi(S/E)$.*"

Accordingly, conditionalization is a function prescribing the value of an agent's credence to be the same as the value of the conditional probability of S (statement) on E (evidence) which is calculated by the following way:

$$P(S/E) = P(S\&E)/P(E)$$

To use this function to calculate the agent's credence, one needs to assume that the probability of the evidence is 1. Such assumptions were widespread in epistemology for a certain period, therefore, it was considered to be a natural intuition concerning learning that new evidence is always certain in the case of learning similar to the way how C.I. Lewis explained the process of learning:

> "If anything is to be probable, then something must be certain. The data which themselves support a genuine probability, must themselves be certainties. We do have such absolute certainties, in the sense data initiating belief and in those passages of experience which later may confirm it." [109:p186]

Lewis' idea, that learning requires the acquaintance of evidence with certainty became rather influential on different fields related to epistemology and decision theory in its time. However, epistemologists and even certain Bayesians soon rushed in to emphasize that Lewis mistakenly requires that for finite epistemic agents, who seldom acquire any evidence will full certainty. Furthermore, it quickly became evident (thanks to Richard Jeffrey's smart example) that the acquaintance of evidence with full certainty is not even a necessary condition for learning as (amongst others) Richard Jeffrey also pointed out. In his example, an agent investigates a piece of cloth by candlelight, and it looks for him green, although he concedes that *"it might be blue or even (but very improbably) violet"*. Let's call these propositions G, B, and V (respectively). Let's say his presupposed probabilities prior the observation of G, B, and V were .30, .30, and .40. After the observation these change to .70, .25, and .05. Now, according to Jeffrey if there was a proposition E of the agent which described *"the precise quality of his visual experience in looking at the cloth, one would say that what the agent learned from the observation was that E is true"* [100:p165] However there need be no proposition E included in his preference ranking. *"Thus, the description "The cloth looked green or possibly blue or conceivably violet," would be too vague to convey the precise quality of the experience."* [100:p165] It would certainly be unwarranted to support such an exact value of conditional probability as those above. *"It seems that the best we can do is to describe, not the quality of the visual experience itself, but rather its effects on the observer, by saying, "After the observation, the agent's degrees of belief in G, B, and V were .70, .25, and .05."* [100:p165-166]

In order to accommodate such cases into our understanding of the learning process, Richard Jeffrey has developed an alternative to classical Bayesian conditionalization which is now called Jeffrey conditionalization. Jeffrey's formula has both of the advantages of fallibilism and Bayesian quantification since it allows calculations of credence and probability with uncertain evidence provided. Consequently, Jeffrey conditionalization avoids the epistemic problems of certainty in determining the probability of a statement, event or states of affairs extending our conception of learning to cases where the learned evidence is still uncertain. Jeffrey defines the probability of the new belief by the following formula:

$$PROBA = prob(A|B)PROBB + probA|(\overline{B})PROB(\overline{B})$$

where PROB A means the agent's credence attributed to belief A after the evidence (PROB B) is acquired and prob (A|B) means the conditional probability of A given B.

As [100, 169-170] explains it, assuming that concerning the conditional probabilities $PROB(A/B)$ and $prob(A/B)$ it is true that $PROB(A/B) = prob(A/B)$ and also it is true that $PROB(A/\overline{B}) = prob(A/\overline{B})$ it is straightforward (given the traditional definition of conditional probability) that

$$PROBA = prob(A|B)PROBB + probA|(\overline{B})PROB(\overline{B}).$$

It is a particular merit of the above formula that it is proven to be Dutch book proof which basically means that irrespective of the input values (given that they fall within the range of 0-1 because they are expressions of probabilities) the output value will also remain between 0-1 and accordingly it is also an expression of probability (cf. [201]). Accordingly, Jeffrey conditionalization can process evidence with any level of certainty which allows the agent to calculate probabilities with uncertain evidence without contradicting Kolmogorov's axioms. Since the level of certainty of a piece of evidence also expresses its epistemic status, using Jeffrey's formula evidence without full epistemic certainty can still serve as the basis of belief update in case of information acquaintance.

14.7 Conclusion

The importance of decision support systems have shown a solid development during the past decades. However, their reasoning framework is still based on rules of Bayesian inference including classic conditionalization which is based on a heavily criticized concept of learning which requires the certainty of evidence. Furthermore, fallibilist epistemologies have pointed out in the last few decades that certainty of evidence is an epistemically problematic concept which is seldom present in real life situations for epistemic agents. Therefore, calculating with certain evidence appears to be hardly applicable which limits the applicability of classic conditionalization. Replacing classic conditionalization with Jeffrey conditionalization allows the system to work with uncertain evidence in accordance with Kolmogorov's axioms. While there are further interesting questions concerning Bayesian probability, such as how to determine prior probability, or how to evaluate the values provided by functions that are based on Bayesian probability theory, these questions are independent from the questions of the certainty of evidence. The above paper only aimed to show that the interpretation of Bayesian probability theory currently applied in a great number of decision support systems is seriously limited. The offered alternative, using Jeffrey conditionalization significantly extends the applicability of the reasoning structure of decision support systems if Bayesian probability theories are at all applicable. For example, for cases where the evidence used by such systems is not entirely certain, the level of certainty attributed to the used evidence can be accommodated to the probability calculations used by the reasoning structure of the system. Without Jeffrey conditionalization this information is lost during such calculations, which causes the system to estimate the probability of an event to be higher or lower than it really is (i.e. it should be estimated according to our present knowledge concerning probability). Since the applicability of Bayesian probability theory is the subject of intense debates, this paper cannot aim for the general assessment of the framework but only for the improvement of its application in decision support systems.

References

[1] S. L. Alter. *Eight Case Studies of Decision Support Systems*. Cambridge, MA: Center for Information Systems Research, Sloan School of Management, MIT, 1974.

[2] D. P. Arnold and A. Michel, editors. *Critical Theory and the Thought of Andrew Feenberg*. New York: Palgrave Macmillan, 2017.

[3] H. Barseghyan and J. Shaw. How can a taxonomy of stances help clarify classical debates on scientific change? *Philosophies*, 2(4):24, 2017. Retrieved from http://www.mdpi.com/2409-9287/2/4/24.

[4] H. Barseghyan. *The Laws of Scientific Change*. New York: Springer, 2015.

[5] J. Baudrillard. Ecran total. *Libération*, page 8, 1996. 6 May.

[6] J. Beniger. *The control revolution: Technological and economic origins of the information society*. Harvard university press, 1986.

[7] P. L. Berger and Th. Luckmann. *The Social Construction of Reality. A Treatise in the Sociology of Knowledge*. New York: Doubleday, 1966.

[8] W. E. Bijker, Th. P. Hughes, and T. Pinch. *The Social Construction of Technological Systems. New Directions in the Sociology and History of Technology*. Cambridge. Mass.: The MIT Press, 1987.

[9] J. Bocharova. The emergence of mind: Personal knowledge and connectionism. *Tradition and Discovery*, 41(3):20–31, 2015. http://polanyisociety.org /TAD

[10] J. Bodini. Immédiation: l'écran comme écart. In J. Bodini M. Carbone, A.C. Dalmasso, editor, *Vivre par(mi) les écrans*, pages 223–242. Les presses du réel, Dijon, 2016.

[11] G. A. Boer. A decision oriented information system. *Journal of Systems Management*, 23(10):36–39, 1972.

[12] J. D. Bolter and R. Grusin. *Remediation: Understanding New Media. 2000*. Cambridge (MA), MIT Press, 2000.

[13] J. D. Bolter. *Turing's Man: Western Culture in the Computer Age*. Chapel Hill: University of North Carolina Press., 1984.

[14] R. H. Bonczek and C. W. Holsappe *Foundations of Decision Support Systems*. Academic Press, 1981.

[15] C. P. Bonini. *Simulation of Information and Decision Systems in the Firm*. Englewood Cliffs,: Prentice Hall., 1963.

[16] A. Borgmann. *Technology and the character of contemporary life: A philosophical inquiry*. University of Chicago Press, 1984.

[17] A. Borgmann. *Crossing the Postmodern Divide*. Chicago: University of Chicago Press., 1992.

[18] A. Borgmann. *Holding on to Reality: The Nature of Information at the Turn of the Millennium*. University of Chicago Press, 1999.

[19] A. Borgmann. *Real American Ethics: Taking Responsibility for Our Country*. University of Chicago Press, 2006.

[20] S. Boxer. Paintings too perfect? the great optics debate. *The New York Times*, 2001. 4 December, http://www.nytimes.com/2001/12/04/arts/paintings-too-perfect-the-great-optics-debate.html.

[21] J. Bundy, M. D. Pfarrer, C. E. Short, and W. T. Coombs. Crises and crisis management: Integration, interpretation, and research development. *Journal of Management*, 43(6):1661–1692, 2016.

[22] M. Bunge. Technology as applied science. *Technology and Culture*, 7, 1966. p. 329-347.

[23] F. Burstein and C. Holsapple, editors. *Handbook on Decision Support Systems*. Springer, 2008.

[24] M. Carbone. *Filosofia-schermi: dal cinema alla rivoluzione digitale*. Raffaello Cortina editore, 2016.

[25] S. Carroll. *Endless Forms Most Beautiful, The New Science of Evo Devo*. New York: W. W. Norton., 2005.

[26] F. Casetti. What is a screen nowadays? In R. Moore C. Berry, J. Harbord, editor, *Public Space. Media Space,*, page 20. Palgrave MacMillan, London, 2013.

[27] M. Castells, G. Cardoso, et al. *The network society: From knowledge to policy*. Johns Hopkins Center for Transatlantic Relations Washington, DC, 2006.

[28] E. Conee and R. Feldman. *Evidentialism*. Oxford: Oxford University Press., 2004.

[29] W. T. Coombs. *Ongoing crisis communication: Planning, managing, and responding*. Sage Publications, 1999.

[30] W. T. Coombs. Crisis communication: A developing field. In R. L. Heath, editor, *The Sage handbook of public relations*, pages 477–488. Sage, 2010.

[31] W. T. Coombs. Parameters for crisis communication. In W. Timothy Coombs and Sherry J Holladay, editors, *The Handbook of Crisis Communication*, pages 17–53. Wiley-Blackwell, 2010.

[32] Cotton Incorporated. The classification of cotton, 2018. Online booklet produced by an industry group working with the approval of and using the standards set up by the US Department of Agriculture. http://www.cottoninc.com/fiber/quality/ Classification-Of-Cotton/Classing-booklet.pdf [accessed January 15, 2018].

[33] R. Dalton. Tempers blaze over artistic integrity, 2006.

[34] G. Deleuze. Plato and the simulacrum. *October*, 27:45–56, 1983. Translated by R. Krauss, appeared at first as G. Deleuze, Renverser le platonisme, "Revue de Métaphysique et de Morale", n. 4, 1967.

[35] G. Deleuze and F. Guattari. *A Thousand Plateaus. Capitalism and Schizophrenia*. Continuum, London - New York, 1980. [201] Translated by B. Massumi.

[36] G. Deleuze. What is a dispositif? In T.J. Armstrong, editor, *Michel Foucault Philosopher*, pages 59–168. Hemel Hempstead, Harvester Wheatsheaf, New York, 1992. ranslated by R. Krauss, appeared at first as G. Deleuze, Renverser le platonisme, "Revue de Métaphysique et de Morale", n. 4, 1967.

[37] G. W. Dickson. Management information decision systems. *Business Horizons*, 11(6):17–26, 1968.

[38] D. A V. Domini. Review of Vermeer's camera and secret knowledge. *Nexus Network Journal*, 4(4), 2002.

[39] M. Druzdezel. *Probabilistic Reasoning in Decision Support Systems: From Computation to Common Sense*. PhD thesis, Carnegie Mellon University., 1993.

[40] A. Dufourcq. *Merleau-Ponty: une ontologie de l'imaginaire*. Springer: Dordrecht-London-New York, 2011.

[41] V. Dusek. *Philosophy of technology: An introduction*, volume 90. Blackwell MaldenOxfordCarlston, 2006.

[42] J. Ellul. *The Technological Society*. New York: Vintage Books, 1964.

[43] S. Eom. The intellectual structure of decision support systems research. In *Decision Support: An Examination of the DSS Discipline*. New York: Springer.szup, 2011. pp. 49-69.

[44] L. Epatko. FBI director recommends 'no charges' over Clinton's email. PBS, 2016. July 15.

[45] P. Érdi. *Complexity Explained*. Berlin, Heidelberg: Springer, 2008.

[46] J. Fantl. Knowledge how. *The Stanford Encyclopedia of Philosophy*, 2017. (Fall 2017 Edition). Retrieved from https://plato.stanford.edu/archives/fall2017/entries/knowledge-how/.

[47] A. Feenberg. *Questioning Technology*. London: Routledge, 1999.

[48] A. Feenberg. *Transforming technology: A critical theory revisited*. Oxford University Press, 2002.

[49] A. Feenberg. Critical theory of technology: An overview. *Tailoring Biotechnologies*, 1(1):47–64, 2005.

[50] A. Feenberg. What is philosophy of technology? In J. R. Dakers, editor, *Defining Technological Literacy*, pages 5–16. New York: Palgrave Macmillan, 2006.

[51] A. Feenberg. *The Philosophy of Praxis: Lukács, Marx and the Frankfort School*. London: Verso, 2016.

[52] A. Feenberg. Replies to critics: Epistemology, ontology, methodology. In D.P. Arnold and A. Michel, editors, *Critical Theory and the Thought of Andrew Feenberg*, pages 285–317. New York: Palgrave Macmillan, 2017.

[53] R. L. Ferguson and C.H. Jones A computer aided decision system. *Management Science*, 15(10):550–561, 1969.

[54] M. Franssen, G.-J. Lokhorst, and I. van de Poel. Philosophy of technology. *The Stanford Encyclopedia of Philosophy*, 2015. (Fall 2015 Edition). Retrieved from https://plato.stanford.edu/archives/fall2015/entries/technology/.

[55] S. Freud. *Beyond the Pleasure Principle*. Penguin, London, 1920. [2003] Translated by J. Reddick.

[56] T. P. J. Gerrity. Design of man-machine decision systems: An application to portfolio management. *Sloan Management Review*, 12(2):59–75, 1971.

[57] E. von Glasersfeld, 2011. http://www.vonglasersfeld.com/ [March 2011].

[58] D. Goehring. The reception of the telescope. *The Astronomy Quarterly*, 2, 1978. pp. 139-152.

[59] A. Goldman. *Epistemology and Cognition.* Cambridge, MA: Harvard University Press., 1986.

[60] E. H. Gombrich. *Art and illusion: A study in the psychology of pictorial representation,* volume 5. Phaedon New York, 1977.

[61] A. González-Herrero and S. Smith. Crisis communications management on the web: how internet-based technologies are changing the way public relations professionals handle business crises. *Journal of Contingencies and Crisis Management,* 16(3):143–153, 2008.

[62] N. Goodman. Languages of art (Indianapolis: Hackett, 1976). *All further references will be cited as" LA,* 1978.

[63] B. Goodwin. Davos: Disintegration of the internet could create economic turmoil. *Computer Weekly,* 2018. http://www.computerweekly.com/news/450433286/Davos-Disintegration-of-the-internet-could-create-economic-turmoil, 17 January.

[64] B. Gopnik. David Stork's uses science to see a world of art through old master's eye's, 2009. Accessed 19 Dec 2017.

[65] M. J. Gorman. Art, optics and history: New light on the Hockney thesis. *Leonardo,* 36(4):295–301, 2003.

[66] R. T. Gould. *The Marine Chronometer, its History and Development.* Woodbridge, Suffolk: Antique Collector's Club, 2013. (2nd ed.).

[67] M. Grene. *The Knower and the Known.* Berkeley: University of CA Press., 1966.

[68] M. Grene. Hobbes and the modern mind. In Marjorie Grene, editor, *The Anatomy of Knowledge: Papers Presented to the Study Group on Foundations of Cultural Unity, Bowdoin College, 1965 and 1966,* pages 1–28. Amherst: University of MA Pres, 1969.

[69] M. Grene, editor. *Knowing and Being: Essays by Michael Polanyi.* Chicago: University of Chicago Press, 1969.

[70] M. Grene, editor. *Toward A Unity of Knowledge. Psychological Issues.* Monograph 22, 6:2., 1969.

[71] M. Grene. Tacit knowing: Grounds for a revolution in philosophy. *Journal of the British Society for Phenomenology,* 8(3):164–171, 1977.

[72] R. Grusin. Radical mediation. *Critical Inquiry,* 42(1):124–148, 2015.

[73] X. Guchet. Théorie du lien social, technologie et philosophie : Simondon lecteur de merleau-ponty. *Les Études philosophiques,* 57:219–237, 2001. 2/2001.

[74] X. Guchet. *Pour un humanisme technologique. Culture, technique et société dans la philosophie de Gilbert Simondon.* Paris, P.U.F., 2010.

[75] M. Guerra and V. Gallese. Embodying movies: Embodied simulation and film studies. *Cinema: Journal of Philosophy and the Moving Image,* 3:183 - 210, 2012.

[76] M. Guerra and V. Gallese. *Lo schermo empatico. Cinema e neuroscienze.* Cortina, Milano, 2015.

[77] M.B.N. Hansen. *Bodies in Code: Interfaces with Digital Media.* New York-London, Routledge, 2006.

[78] M. G. Haselton, D. Nettle, and D. R. Murray. The evolution of cognitive bias. *The handbook of evolutionary psychology*, 2005.

[79] M. Héder and D. Paksi. Autonomous robots and tacit knowledge. *Appraisal*, 9(2):8–14, 2012.

[80] M. Héder. Michael Polanyi and the epistemology of engineering. In *Proceedings of BudPT2017*, 2018.

[81] M. Héder and D. Paksi. Non-human knowledge according to Michael Polanyi. *Tradition and Discovery: The Polanyi Society Periodical*, 44(1):50–66, 2018.

[82] M. Heidegger. *What is a Thing?* South Bend, Indiana: Gateway Editions, 1967. Translated by W. B. Barton Jr. and V. Deutsch.

[83] M. Heidegger. *The Question Concerning Technology and Other Essays*. New York & London: Garland Publishing, 1977. Translated and with an Introduction by William Lovitt.

[84] A. van Helden. The telescope and cosmic dimensions. In R Taton and C Wilson, editors, *The General History of Astronomy. Volume 2: Planetary Astronomy from the Renaissance to the Rise of Astrophysics. Part A: Tycho Brahe to Newton*, pages 106–118. 1989. [2003].

[85] A. van Helden. Telescopes and authority from Galileo to Cassini. *Osiris*, 9, 1994. pp. 8-29.

[86] D. Hill. *A History of Engineering in Classical and Medieval Times*. London, New York: Routledge, 1996.

[87] R. Hilpinen. Artifact. In Edward N. Zalta, editor, *The Stanford Encyclopedia of Philosophy (Winter 2011 Edition)*. 2011. https://plato.stanford.edu/archives/win2011/entries/artifact/.

[88] D. Hockney. Secret Knowledge: Rediscovering the lost techniques of the old masters. *New York: Viking Studio*, 2001.

[89] E. Hörl. Prostheses of desire: on bernard Stiegler's new critique of projection. *Parrhesia*, 20:10, 2014. Translated by A.D. Boever.

[90] S.-C. Hung and J.-Y. Lai. When innovations meet chaos: Analyzing the technology development of printers in 1976–2012. *Journal of Engineering and Technology Management*, 42:31–45, 2016.

[91] D. Hurley. Can an algorithm tell when kids are in danger? *New York Times*, 2018. https://nyti.ms/2EzTlpC, 2 January.

[92] D. Ihde and E. Selinger, editors. *Chasing Technoscience. Matrix for Materiality*. Bloomington & Indianapolis: Indiana U. P, 2003.

[93] D. Ihde. *Technics and praxis*. Dordrecht: Reidel Publishing Company, 1979.

[94] D. Ihde. *Technology and the Lifeworld: From Garden to Earth*. Indianapolis: Indiana University Press, 1990.

[95] D. Ihde. *Philosophy of Technology: An Introduction*. New York: Paragon House, 1993.

[96] D. Ihde. *Heidegger's Technologies. Postphenomenological Perspectives*. New York: Fordham University Press, 2010.

[97] D. Ihde. Art precedes science: or did the camera obscura invent modern science? instruments in art and science: On the architectonics of cultural boundaries in the 17th century vol 2 engl. edn ed j lazardzig et al, 2008.

[98] J.M. Jacques, L. Gatot, and A. Wallemacq. A cognitive approach to crisis management in organizations. *International handbook of organizational crisis management*, pages 161–193, 2007.

[99] R. C. Jeffrey. *The Logic of Decision*. University of Chicago Press, 1983.

[100] R. Jeffrey. *The Logic of Decision*. University of Chicago Press., 1965.

[101] R. Jeffrey. *Subjective probability the real thing*. Cambridge: Cambridge University Press., 2004.

[102] W. A. Kahn, M. A. Barton, and S. Fellows. Organizational crises and the disturbance of relational systems. *Academy of Management Review*, 38(3):377–396, 2013.

[103] K. Kavoulakos. Philosophy of praxis or philosophical anthropology? Andrew Feenberg and Axel Honneth on Lukács's theory of reification. In D.P. Arnold and A. Michel, editors, *Critical Theory and the Thought of Andrew Feenberg*, pages 47–69. New York: Palgrave Macmillan, 2017.

[104] W.R. King and D.I. Cleland. Decision and information systems for strategic planning. *Business Horizons*, 16:29–36, 1973.

[105] C. Kuang. Can a.i. be taught to explain itself? *New York Times Magazine*, pages 46–53, 2017. 26 November.

[106] C. Lawson. Feenberg, rationality and isolation. In D.P. Arnold and A. Michel, editors, *Critical Theory and the Thought of Andrew Feenberg*, pages 91–113. New York: Palgrave Macmillan, 2017.

[107] J. Law. Technology and heterogeneous engineering: The case of Portuguese expansion. In Wiebe E. Bijker, Thomas P. Hughes, and Trevor Pinch, editors, *The Social Construction of Technological Systems. New Directions in the Sociology and History of Technology*, pages 111–134. Cambridge. Mass.: The MIT Press, 1987.

[108] O. Lerbinger. *The crisis manager: Facing risk and responsibility*. Lawrence Erlbaum Associates, 1997.

[109] C. I. Lewis. *An Analysis of Knowledge and Valuation*. La Salle, Illinois: Open Court., 1946.

[110] J. D. C. Little. Models and managers: The concepts of a decision calculus. *Management Science*, 16(8):466–485, 1970.

[111] S. Lojkine, editor. *L'écran de la représentation*. L'Harmattan, Paris, 2001.

[112] C. Lotz. Gegenständlichkeit - from Marx to Lukács and back again. In D.P. Arnold and A. Michel, editors, *Critical Theory and the Thought of Andrew Feenberg*, pages 71–89. New York: Palgrave Macmillan, 2017.

[113] J. F. Lyotard. *Dérive á partir de Marx et Freud*. Galilée, 1994.

[114] J. F. Lyotard. *Des dispositifs pulsionnels*. Galilée, 1994.

[115] J.-F. Lyotard. Freud according to cézanne. *Parrhesia*, pages 26–42, 1973. Translated by A. Woodward, J. Roffe.

[116] K. Marx. *Introduction to a Contribution to a Critique of Political Economy*. Manuscript, 1857.

https://www.marxists.org/archive/marx/works/1859/critique-pol-economy/appx1.htm#195.

[117] M. Mauss. Les techniques du corps. *Journal de Psychologie*, 32(3-4), 1936. Repris in Techniques, technologie et civilisation, sous la direction de N. Schlanger, Paris: PUF, 365-394; English translation : "Techniques of the Body", in Techniques, Technology and Civilization, New York/Oxford: Durkheim Press/Berghahn Books, 2006, 77-96.

[118] W. Mazzarella. Internet x-ray: E-governance, transparency, and the politics of immediation in india. *Public Culture*, 18(3):473–505, 2006.

[119] C.L. Meador and D.N. Ness. Decision support system: An application to corporate planning. *Sloan Management Review*, 15(2):51–68, 1974.

[120] E. Meek. *Contact with Reality: Michael Polanyi's Realism and Why It Matters*. Eugene, OR: Cascade, OR., 2017.

[121] M. Merleau-Ponty. *La structure du comportement*. Paris: PUF, 2002, 1942. [1942] English trans.: Alden Fisher, The Structure of Behavior, Pittsburgh: Duquesne University Press, 1983.

[122] M. Merleau-Ponty. *Phénoménologie de la perception*. Paris: Gallimard, 1945. [1992] English translation by C. Smith, Phenomenology of Perception, London: Routledge, 2005 (PhP).

[123] M. Merleau-Ponty. *Le cinéma et la nouvelle psychologie*. 1947. [1964] English translation : H. Dreyfus and P. Dreyfus,"The Film and the New Psychology", in *Sense and Non-Sense*, Evanston: Northwestern University Press, 1964.

[124] M. Merleau-Ponty. *L'aeil et l'esprit*. Paris: Gallimard, 1964. English translation edited by L. Lawlor and T. Toadvine, "Eye and Mind", in *The Merleau-Ponty Reader*, Evanston: Northwestern University Press, 2007, 359 (EM).

[125] M. Merleau-Ponty. La philosophie aujourd'hui. Cours de 1958-1959. In *Notes de cours. 1959-1961*. Text established by S. Ménasé, Paris : Gallimard, 1996.

[126] M. Merleau-Ponty. *Le monde sensible et le monde de l'expression*. Text established by E. de Saint Aubert and S. Kristensen, Genéve, MetisPresses, 2011.

[127] M. Mirkin. The status of technological knowledge in the scientific mosaic. *Scientonomy*, 2, 2018. forthcoming.

[128] C. Mitcham. *Thinking through Technology. The Path between Engineering and Philosophy*. Chicago: University of Chicago Press, 1994.

[129] P. Montani. Ma google glass è uno schermo? *Rivista di estetica*, 55:169–182, 2014.

[130] D. Montogmery and G. Urban. Marketing decision-information systems: An emerging view. *Journal of Marketing Research*, 7(2):226 - 234, 1970.

[131] S. Morton. *Management Support Systems: Computer Based Support for Decision Making*. Cambridge, MA: Division of Research, Harvard University, 1971.

[132] E. Muir. *The Culture Wars of the Late Renaissance*. Harvard University Press., 2007.

[133] S. Mukherjee. This cat sensed death. what if computers could, too? *The New York Times*, 2018.

https://www.nytimes.com/2018/01/03/magazine/the-dying-algorithm.html, 3 January.

[134] Ph. Mullins. The fluid word: Word processing and its mental habits. *Thought: Fordham University Quarterly*, 63:413–428, 1988.

[135] Ph. Mullins. Media ecology and the new literacy: Notes on an electronic hermeneutic. In Paul A. Soukup and Robert Hodgson, editors, *From One Medium to Another: Basic Issues for Communicating the Scriptures in New Media*, pages 310–333. Kansas City: Sheed and Ward, 1997.

[136] Ph. Mullins. The real as meaningful. *Tradition and Discovery*, 26(3):42–50, 2000. http://polanyisociety.org/TAD50-pdf.

[137] Ph. Mullins. Comprehension and the 'comprehensive entity': Polanyi's theory of tacit knowing and its metaphysical implications. *Tradition and Discovery*, 33(3):26–43, 2007. http://polanyisociety.org/TAD43-pdf.

[138] Ph. Mullins. Michael Polanyi's approach to biological systems and contemporary biosemiotics. *Tradition and Discovery*, 43(1):5–37, 2017. http://polanyisociety.org/ TAD

[139] Ph. Mullins. Michael Polanyi on machines as comprehensive entities, 2018.

[140] Ph. Mullins. Polanyi's participative realism. *Polanyiana*, 6(2):5–21, 1997. http://www.polanyi.bme.hu/folyoirat/1997-02/1997- 11-polanyis_participative_realism.pdf [accessed December 24, 2017].

[141] S. L. Myers and E. Lichtblau. Hillary Clinton is criticized for private emails in state dept. review. *The New York Times*, 2016. May 26, 2016.

[142] F. Nietzsche. *Twilight of the Idols or How to Philosophize with a Hammer*. Oxford University Press, Oxford, 2013. Translated by D. Large.

[143] F. Nietzsche. *The Gay Science*. Cambridge University Press, Cambridge, 2001. Preface to the Second Edition, edited by B. Williams, translated by J. Nauckhoff, 2001, p. 8.

[144] M. Nijhuis. Vous avez dit écrans? entre miroir et voile, le voile prismatique. In J. Bodini M. Carbone, A.C. Dalmasso, editor, *Vivre par(mi) les écrans*, pages 113–133. Les presses du réel, Dijon, 2016.

[145] I. Nonaka and H. Takeuchi. *The Knowledge-Creating Company*. New York: Oxford University Press, 1995.

[146] M. J. Nye. *Michael Polanyi and His Generation*. Chicago: University of Chicago Press, 2011.

[147] R. Jr. O'Harrow. How Clinton's email scandal took root. *The Washington Post*, 2016. March 27, 2016.

[148] J. K. B. Olsen, S. A. Pedersen, and V. F. Hendricks, editors. *A Companion to the Philosophy of Technology*. Chichester: Wiley Blackwell, 2009.

[149] J. K. B. Olsen, E. Selinger, and S. Riis. *New Waves in Philosophy of Technology*. New York: Palgrave Macmillan, 2009.

[150] P. Patton, N. Overgaard, and H. Barseghyan. Reformulating the second law. *Scientonomy*, 1, 2017. pp. 29-39. Retrieved from http://www.scientojournal.com/index.php/scientonomy/article/view/27158.

[151] PBS Digital Studio. Crash course computer science, 2018. 41 episodes, https://www.youtube.com/watch?v=O5nskjZ_GoI [accessed January 7, 2018].

[152] R. Perkins. Technological "lock-In". *Internet Encyclopaedia of Ecological Economics*, 2003.

[153] D. C. Perry, M. Taylor, and M. L. Doerfel. Internet-based communication in crisis management. *Management communication quarterly*, 17(2):206–232, 2003.

[154] J. V. Pickstone. *Ways of Knowing. A New History of Science, Technology and Medicine*. Chicago: The University of Chicago Press, 2001.

[155] T. J. Pinch and W. E. Bijker. The social construction of facts and artefacts: Or how the sociology of science and the sociology of technology might benefit each other. *Social Studies of Science*, 13(3):399–441, 1984.

[156] D. G. Pintér. A vállalat felelősségvállalásától az érdekgazdák észleléséig: a szituációs kríziskommunikációs elmélet és a kommunikációs keretezés elmélet kapcsolódási pontjainak feltárása a válságkommunikáció módszertanának fejlesztése céljából *JelKép*, 3:34–52, 2016.

[157] D. G. Pintér. Media bias and the role of user generated contents in crisis management: a case-study about the communication of the hungarian police forces after 2016 budapest explosion. *Corvinus Journal of Sociology and Social Policy*, 2018.

[158] D. G. Pintér. Public self-demolition in practice: The conclusions of the crisis communication of the children cancer foundation from the perspective of public relations. *Periodica Polytechnica. Social and Management Sciences*, 24(1):41, 2016.

[159] D. G. Pintér. Various challenges of science communication in teaching generation z: an urgent need for paradigm shift and embracing digital learning. *Opus et Educatio*, 3(6), 2016.

[160] J. C. Pitt. *Thinking About Technology*. New York: Seven Bridges Press, 2000.

[161] M. Polanyi. *Gifford Lectures*. Polanyi Society, 1952. Held in 1951-52 "An Introduction to Michael Polanyi's Gifford Lectures" and "Syllabus for Series I" http://www.polanyisociety.org/Giffords/Giffords-web-page9-20-16.htm.

[162] M. Polanyi. The hypothesis of cybernetics. *British Journal for the Philosophy of Science*, 2(8):312–315, 1952.

[163] M. Polanyi. Skills and connoisseurship. *Atti del Congressor di studi methodological promosso dal Cntro di studi methodologi*, pages 381–394, 1952. Torino (17-20 dicembre).

[164] M. Polanyi. *The Study of Man*. Chicago: University of Chicago Press, 1959.

[165] M. Polanyi. Knowing and being. *Mind*, 71:458–470, 1961. Grene, *Knowing and Being: Essays by Michael Polanyi*: 123-137.

[166] M. Polanyi. Tacit knowing: Its bearing on some problems in philosophy. *Review of Modern Physics*, 36(4):601–616, 1962. Also in Philosophy Today, 6:4: 239-262 and, in abbreviated form, in Grene, Knowing and Being: Essays by Michael Polanyi: 159-180.

[167] M. Polanyi. Duke lectures, 1964. http://www.polanyisociety.org/Duke-intro.htm.

[168] M. Polanyi. On the modern mind. *Encounter*, 24:12–20, 1965.

[169] M. Polanyi. The structure of consciousness. *Brain*, 88:799–810, 1965. Also in Grene, *Knowing and Being: Essays by Michael Polanyi*: 225-239.

[170] M. Polanyi. Wesleyan lectures, 1965. http://www.polanyisociety.org/WesleyanLectures/WesleyanLecturesIntro.htm.

[171] M. Polanyi. Interviews of Polanyi by Ray Wilken. Wesleyan Interview Transcript 3 File, 1966. (April 5 and 6, pp. 9-10), http://www.polanyisociety.org/WilkenInterview/WslynIntrvwApr5&6-1966-transcript-file3.pdf.

[172] M. Polanyi. The logic of tacit inference. *Philosophy*, 41:1–18, 1966. Also in Grene, *Knowing and Being: Essays by Michael Polanyi*: 138-158.

[173] M. Polanyi. *The Tacit Dimension*. Garden City, New York: Doubleday and Co, Inc., 1966.

[174] M. Polanyi. Life's irreducible structure. *Science*, 160:1309–1312, 1968. Also in Grene, Knowing and Being: Essays by Michael Polanyi: 225-239.

[175] M. Polanyi. *Personal Knowledge, Towards a Post-Critical Philosophy*. Chicago: University of Chicago Press [1958]. New York: Harper Torchbooks [1964], 1958.

[176] D. Pritchard. *What is this Thing Called Knowledge?* Routledge., 2010.

[177] D. Pritchard. Virtue epistemology and epistemic luck, revisited. *Metaphilosophy*, 39(1):66–88, 2008.

[178] H. Radder. Critical philosophy of technology: The basic issues. *Social Epistemology*, 22:51–70, 2008.

[179] W. Rawleigh. The status of questions in the ontology of scientific change. *Scientonomy*, 2, 2018. pp. 1-12. Retrieved from https://scientojournal.com/index.php/scientonomy/article/view/29651.

[180] G. Rizzolatti, V. Gallese and C. Keysers. A unifying view of the basis of social cognition. *Trends in Cognitive Sciences*, 9:396 - 403, 2004.

[181] A. R. Roberts. Assessment, crisis intervention, and trauma treatment: The integrative act intervention model. *Brief treatment and crisis intervention*, 2(1):1–22, 2006.

[182] L. Ropolyi. The "science = technology + philosophy" thesis. In S. Kaneva, editor, *Challenges Facing Philosophy In United Europe*, pages 39–49. Sofia: IPhR - BAS, 2004.

[183] L. Ropolyi. Technika és etika. In L. Fekete, editor, *Kortárs etika*, pages 245–292. Budapest: Nemzeti Tankönyvkiadó, 2004.

[184] L. Ropolyi. *Philosophy of the Internet. A Discourse on the Nature of the Internet*. Budapest: Eötvös Lóránd University, 2013. http://www.tankonyvtar.hu/en/tartalom/tamop412A/2011-0073_philosophy_of_the_Internet/adatok.html.

[185] L. Ropolyi. On the science-technology relationship: a historical view. In H. de Regt and C. Kwa, editors, *Building Bridges. Connecting Science, Technology and Philosophy*, pages 175–187. Amsterdam: VU University Press, 2014.

[186] L. Ropolyi. *Az Internet természete. Internetfilozófiai értekezés.* Budapest: Typotex, 2006. (in Hungarian. "On the Nature of the Internet. Discourse on the Philosophy of the Internet").

[187] S. D. Ross. *A theory of art: Inexhaustibility by contrast.* SUNY Press, 1982.

[188] C. Roux-Dufort. Is crisis management (only) a management of exceptions? *Journal of contingencies and crisis management,* 15(2):105–114, 2007.

[189] G. Ryle. *The Concept of Mind.* Chicago: The University of Chicago Press, 1949.

[190] Y. Saghai. Salvaging the concept of nudge. *Journal of medical ethics,* 39(8):487–493, 2013.

[191] E. de Saint Aubert. *Être et chair. Du corps au désir: l'habilitation ontologique de la chair.* Paris : Vrin, 2013.

[192] R. C. Scharff and V. Dusek, editors. *Philosophy of Technology. The Technological Condition: An Anthology.* Chichester: Wiley Blackwell, 2014. Second Edition.

[193] P. Schilder. *The image and Appearance of the Human Body.* Kegan Paul, Trench, Trubner & Co., London, 1935.

[194] R. A. Seaberg and C. Seaberg. Computer based decision systems in xerox corporate planning. *Management Science,* 20(4):575 - 584, 1973.

[195] Z. Sebastien. The status of normative propositions in the theory of scientific change. *Scientonomy,* 1, 2016. pp. 1-9. Retrieved from http://www.scientojournal.com/index.php/scientonomy/article/view/26947.

[196] M. W. Seeger, T. L. Sellnow, and R. R. Ulmer. Communication, organization, and crisis. *Annals of the International Communication Association,* 21(1):231–276, 1998.

[197] Yan Q. Shan, S. *Emergency Response Decision Support System.* Singapore: Springer., 2017.

[198] G. Simondon. *Du mode d'existence des objets techniques.* Paris: Aubier, 1969. [2012] English translation by C. Malaspina and J. Rogove, *On the Mode of Existence of Technical Objects,* Minneapolis: Univocal Publishing, 2016.

[199] G. Simondon. Sur la technoesthétique, 1982. Draft for a letter to Jacques Derrida, 3rd July 1982, Les Papiers du Collége International de Philosophie 1992/12; then republished with some "Suppléments" as "Réflexions sur la techno-esthétique". In *Sur la technique,* 392 - 96 (STE). Paris: PUF, 2014 ; English translation: A. De Boever, "On Techno-Aesthetics".Parrhesia 2012/14: 1 - 8 https://www.parrhesiajournal.org/parrhesia14/parrhesia14_simondon.pdf (OTA, not numbered).

[200] G. Simondon. *L'individuation á la lumiére des notions de forme et d'information.* Paris: Millon, 2005.

[201] B. Skyrms. Dynamic coherence and probability kinematics. *Philosophy of Science,* 54(1):1–20, 1987.

[202] B. Skyrms. *Choice and Chance: An Introduction to Inductive Logic.* Cengage Learning, 1999.

[203] V. Sobchack. The scene of the screen. In *Carnal thoughts. Embodiement and moving image culture,* pages 135–178. University of California Press, Berkeley and Los Angeles, California, 2004.

[204] D. Sobel. *The Illustrated Longitude: The True Story of the Lone Genius Who Solved the Greatest Scientific Problem of His Time.* New York: Walker & Company, 1998.

[205] E. Sosa. The raft and the pyramid: Coherence versus foundations in the theory of knowledge. *Midwest Studies in Philosophy*, 5(1):3–26, 1980.

[206] E. Sosa. *Apt Belief and Reflective Knowledge, Volume I.: A virtue epistemology.* Oxford: Oxford University Press., 2007.

[207] E. Sosa. *Apt Belief and Reflective Knowledge, Volume II: Reflective Knowledge.* Oxford: Oxford University Press., 2009.

[208] A. S. Spooner. Mathematical foundations of decision support systems. In E. S. Berner, editor, *Clinical Decision Support Systems Theory and Practice.* New York: Springer, 2016. pp. 19 - 45.

[209] R. H. J. Sprague. A framework for the development of decision support systems. *MIS Quarterly*, 4(4):1–26, 1980.

[210] B. Stiegler. *Technics and Time, 1. The Fault of Epimetheus.* Standford University Press, Redwood City, California, 1998. Translated by R. Beardsworth, G. Collins.

[211] B. Stiegler. *Technics and Time, 3. Cinematic Time and the Question of Malaise.* Standford University Press, Redwood City, California, 2010. Translated by S. Barker.

[212] W. Talbott. Bayesian epistemology. *The Stanford Encyclopedia of Philosophy*, 2016. https://plato.stanford.edu/archives/win2016/entries/epistemology-bayesian/ Winter 2016.

[213] J. Tanács and G. Zemplén. Válság, kommunikáció, érvelés: Kríziskommunikáció argumentáció-elméleti nézőpontból *JelKép*, 2:1–14, 2015.

[214] R. H. Thaler, C. R. Sunstein, and J. P. Balz. Choice architecture. *SSRN*, 2010. Available at : https://ssrn.com/abstract=1583509.

[215] R. H. Thaler and C. R. Sunstein. *Nudge: Improving Decisions about Health, Wealth and Happiness.* Yale University Press, 2006.

[216] V. Thoren. Tycho Brahe. In R Taton and C Wilson, editors, *The General History of Astronomy. Volume 2: Planetary Astronomy from the renaissance to the rise of astrophysics. Part A: Tycho Brahe to Newton*, pages 3–21. Cambridge: Cambridge University Press, 1989. [2003].

[217] J. Toobin. Hillary's problem: The government classifies everything. *The New Yorker*, 2015. August 18.

[218] A. Tversky and D. Kahneman. Judgments under uncertainty: Heuristics and biases. *Science*, 185(4157):1124 - 1131, 1974.

[219] M. A. Vasarhelyi. Man-machine planning systems: A cognitive style examination of interactive decision making. *Journal of Accounting Research*, 15(1):138 - 153, 1977.

[220] S. J. Venette. Risk communication in a high reliability organization. *Ann Arbor, MI: UMI Proquest Information and Learning*, 2003.

[221] W. A. Vincenti. *What Engineers Know and How They Know It: Analytical Studies from Aeronautical History.* Baltimore, MD/London: Johns Hopkins University Press, 1990.

References

[222] S. Vogel. What is the "philosophy of praxis"? In D.P. Arnold and A. Michel, editors, *Critical Theory and the Thought of Andrew Feenberg*, pages 17– 45. New York: Palgrave Macmillan, 2017.

[223] M. Weber. Science as a vocation. In *Science and the Quest for Reality*, pages 382–394. Springer, 1946.

[224] J. Williamson and G. Wheeler. Evidential probability and objective Bayesian epistemology. In *Philosophy of Statistics*, page 307 - 331. Elsevier, 2011.

[225] L. Jr. White. *Medieval Technology and Social Change*. Oxford: Oxford University Press, 2010.

[226] E. Whitney. *Paradise Restored: The Mechanical Arts from Antiquity Through the Thirteenth Century*. Philadelphia: American Philosophical Society, 1990.

[227] J. Williamson. Deliberation, judgement and the nature of evidence. *Economics and Philosophy*, 31, 2015.

[228] U. A. Yajnik. Reflections on James Bond of AI. *AI & Society*, 2017. https://doi.org/10.1007/s00146-017- 0770-z [accessed January 3, 2018].

[229] S. Zizek. *Organs Without Bodies. On Deleuze and Consequences*. Routledge, New Yord - London, 2004.

[230] S. Zizek. *How to Read Lacan*. Granta Books, London, 2006.

Index

A

aesthetic thinking 93-95
Albert Borgmann 25, 61, 105, 115-121, 130

B

Bayesian conditionalization 135-136
Black Mirror 75-76, 81, 86
boundary conditions 45, 50, 60

C

camera lucida 110-111, 114
camera obscura 109, 111
Caravaggio 109, 111
Charles Falco 109, 110
coherentism 144
comprehensive biotic entities 36, 39-40, 49-52, 60
comprehensive entity 36, 38, 39-40
contrivance 35, 38, 61, 68
crisis 104-105, 123-126
Critical Theory 22

D

Daniel Kahneman 115, 118
David Hockney 109, 110
deceptive substitution 59
decision support system (DSS) 135-138
Deleuze 76, 79, 82, 84
determinism 22, 23, 49, 110-111
device paradigm 105, 115, 123, 133
disorganisation 76, 84-85
Duke lectures 40, 46, 49

E

Ellul 20, 22
email controversy 131
epistemic stances 5, 8
explicable 7, 12
explicable-implicit 10-11

F

Feenberg 3, 19, 22, 51, 112
fiduciary program 40, 41, 43, 53-54, 65
foundationalism 144
Frankfurt School 23

G

Gifford lectures 48, 54
glamour 117-118
Guattari 76, 84-86

H

Heidegger 3, 20, 22-23, 29, 42, 51, 85
heuristic passion 35, 63, 68-69
Hillary Clinton 131-132
Hockney-Falco thesis 109, 113
Human Praxis 19, 27
hyperreal 61, 105, 116-121
Hypothesis of Cybernetics 53-54

I

ideology of absolute transparency 78-79, 80, 82
immediation 80-81
implicit 3, 5, 7, 9-11, 30
inexplicable 7, 10-11
infallibilism 145
instrumentalism 22-23
intellectual passions 68

J

Jeffrey conditionalization 135, 147

K

Kolmogorov's axioms 148

L

Life's Irreducible Structure 50, 64

M

machine learning 59-60
Merleau-Ponty 42, 74, 89, 90, 96
Michael Polanyi 10, 35-40, 49-51, 54-56, 60, 64-69
moral inversion 65

N

non-propositional knowledge 11
nudging 106, 115, 120-121

O

ontology of scientific change 6-8
operational principles 48, 52, 64, 66-68
opting for no control 116, 118, 120
ordering principles 35, 39, 66

P

personal coefficient 64
personal knowledge 63, 64 65
persuasive passion 68
polyvalent dimensions 41, 42
post-critical [philosophy] 33, 35-36, 40, 56, 64
principle of derepresentation 81
propositional knowledge 11-12

R

regime of light 82

S

scientonomy 5-6, 8-9, 11, 14
selective passion 68
self-driving vehicle 116-118
Simondon 74, 84, 90, 94-95
social construction of technology (SCOT) 25, 30,
substantivism 22-23

T

techno-aesthetics 89, 90, 91, 94, 97
technological knowledge 3, 5, 7-8
Thaler 106, 112
theory acceptance 6, 8
theory use 8
The Tacit Dimension 39, 45

U

uncertainty problem 146

V

verisimilitude 110-112

Z

Žižek 85

www.ingramcontent.com/pod-product-compliance
Lightning Source LLC
Chambersburg PA
CBHW052049300426
44117CB00012B/2039